VIL

NO REMORSE III

by

Al McIntosh

with Dean Rinaldi

Published by Blue Mendos Publications
In association with Amazon KDP

Published in paperback 2023
Category: Memoirs & Life Story
Copyright Al McIntosh © 2023
ISBN : 9798861207638u

Cover design by Jill Rinaldi © 2023

Dedication

To my granddaughter, my English Rose, Emily-Rose.

Acknowledgements

Jill Rinaldi for my book covers & my good friend and

Ghostwriter, Dean Rinaldi.

A Message from Al McIntosh

I first met Reg Kray while serving time at HMP Parkhurst as we were both prisoners on C wing during the 1980s. I can tell you nothing about his life of crime or his personal life. We chatted on numerous occasions, but it would be wrong for me to suggest that we were friends; only fellow inmates serving time. Reg Kray was a quiet man and I enjoyed our brief conversations. I never witnessed him raise his voice or raise a hand to another prisoner. In my opinion, he could, at times, appear extremely sad. I could only imagine that the weight of his enormous prison sentence must have crushed his soul day by day, month by month and year by year. In all honesty, I admired his bravery and the way he dealt with managing that terrible sentence. The other inmates and I had hope to keep us going through the difficult times, because the day, no matter how far away, would arrive when we could leave as free men who had paid their hefty debt to society.

Chapter 1

Al could feel his legs giving way as kick after kick connected.

"I'm losing, I'm fucking losing," Al thought as the mass of angry boots battered his body.

Al's legs collapsed from under him. His face and body suffered punch after punch.

"I can't punch... I'm going down," Al thought as he lay on the cold tile floor.

With *'The Tide is High'* by Blondie booming out of the speakers, Black Sandra screamed at the top of her voice for the mob to stop, while frantically rummaging through her handbag.

"This is it... the end... I'm going to die," Al thought as two Leicester lads whacked, hammered and pummelled his limp body with their pickaxe handles.

"Leave him alone!" Black Sandra shouted as she gripped her Beretta handgun tightly.

The Leicester Mob continued their merciless, unabated, and vicious attack on Al.

Black Sandra dropped her handbag and held the gun in both hands.

"Stop... You're killing him!"

BANG! BANG! BANG!

Black Sandra fired the handgun. The Leicester lads ducked and cowered before racing out of the amusement arcade. Black Sandra stood firm, legs apart, holding the lethal weapon.

Black Sandra was an active prostitute who worked the Kings Cross area. She enjoyed adventurous liaisons with both men and women. There had always been an unspoken chemistry between Black Sandra and Al, but it was only after Al had helped her and her flatmate by slapping two overly ambitious debt collectors, that Black Sandra announced to Al that she'd like their relationship to progress beyond friends. She was very clear what the rules were. There were to be no expectations, no commitment and no jealousy from either party. Al wholeheartedly agreed to the friends with benefits arrangement.

Black Sandra had bought herself a handgun after she was raped and badly beaten by a punter. She would often walk the streets of Kings Cross late at night in the hope of meeting up with the rapist. She was prepared to take his life and serve whatever time came with the street justice.

The very lucrative Kings Cross area was under the control of Al McIntosh and his trusted circle of friends. It had been a bloody, violent, and savage rise, but the rewards far outweighed any of the danger. With such prime pickings, a team of motivated and extremely violent lads from Leicester decided that they were going to take it by any and all means possible. They didn't expect the criminals to band together after they tore the nipple from a working girl on the streets. With the Leicester lads beaten and sent running, Al knew it was only a matter of time before there would be some kind of retaliation. Al and Black Sandra were at the pub planning a foursome with two stunningly attractive punk rockers,

Fliss and Debs, when Al had to leave to discuss business with a friend at the amusement arcade. The Leicester lads were tooled up and waiting.

Black Sandra slowly lowered the gun and looked down at Al's beaten and crumpled body.

"Al, are you okay?" Black Sandra whispered as she rubbed his shoulder.

"You need to get away from here," Al murmured, wincing with pain.

"I'll get an ambulance."

"No, run!" Al persisted. "The police will be here soon. Get rid of the shooter."

Black Sandra looked down at the gun and promptly put it back in her bag.

"Are you sure?"

"Run!" Al cried out.

"The bastards nearly killed me," Al thought as a tingling sensation washed over his entire body.

Al watched as Black Sandra stood up, smiled awkwardly and then bolted towards the exit.

"This isn't good," Al thought as he tried to move.

He managed to lift himself just a few inches before slumping back down onto the tiled floor.

Nee Naw…Nee Naw…Nee Naw.

Al recognised the sound of police sirens. He closed his eyes and allowed his face to rest on the cold floor tiles.

SNIFF… SNIFF…

"They've come back to kill me," Al thought before opening his eyes to find a police dog sniffing his face.

"The old bill, fuck, are they going to set that fucking dog on me?" Al thought as he struggled to manage the excruciating pain from his chest, arms and back.

"Those black bastards got you then Al," one of the police officers said, shaking his head.

Al tried again to move, but the pain was too much.

"Stay where you are lad," a second police officer said. "There's an ambulance on the way."

"Was it those black slags from Leicester?" the first officer said through gritted teeth. "Just give us the nod and we'll nick each and every last one of them."

Al remained quiet.

"They discharged a firearm. That will get them big time," the officer continued.

"I might hate the bastards for who they are and what they did, but I ain't no grass," Al thought as he closed his eyes.

"Out of the way!"

Al opened his eyes to see two paramedics carrying a stretcher.

"How fucking bad am I?" Al thought as the pain surged in short, sharp, waves through his body.

The paramedics carried the stretcher back to the ambulance. The first police officer followed them.

"Just give us the word and we'll nick those bastards!" the officer shouted just before the ambulance door was slammed shut.

"I'm no fucking grass," Al thought as the ambulance raced across London to the Royal Northern Hospital on the Holloway Road. *"How do these racist bastards even get into the old bill?"*

Al was rushed from the ambulance and into the hospital. He drifted in and out of consciousness as they X-Rayed his body and bound the broken and fractured bones. Al was then moved to a ward where he fell into a deep, dreamless, sleep.

***

"Good morning Mr McIntosh," a young male doctor with a receding hairline said, while reading the notes at the bottom of Al's bed.

"Good morning."

"How do you feel?"

"Like I've been run over by a steam roller," Al said, struggling for breath.

The doctor chuckled and placed the note pad back onto the base of the bed.

"What happened to you?"

"I was mugged," Al replied.

"Well, they were very clearly dangerous people," the doctor said. "You have two broken ribs, a broken thumb and a fractured cheek bone."

"Is that it?" Al thought.

"In all my years in medicine I have never, ever witnessed bodily bruising to the extent you've endured."

"That explains the pain," Al thought as he gasped for breath.

"We've checked your lungs and luckily for you they're not punctured, but you will have to take it easy and rest your body.

Al smiled.

"Thank you doctor."

It was shortly after midday when Al perked up as Black Sandra approached the hospital bed.

"Are you going to be okay?"

Al smiled and nodded.

"Did you get rid of it?" Al whispered.

Black Sandra looked left and then right before replying.

"I dumped it in Regents Canal."

"Good," Al replied. "Having a shooter carries instant jail time."

"I'll get another," Black Sandra said. "This is London after all."

Al struggled to chuckle and then gasped for breath.

"Those bastards were going to kill you," Black Sandra said.

"Yeah, and thanks to you it didn't happen."

"It's what friends do."

"Good friends," Al replied.

"So, what happened with Fliss and Debs, the two punk rocker birds?"

"Fuck it," Black Sandra said. "I forgot all about them."

"Yeah, I bet you had the pair of them," Al said with a wry grin.

"They were both right up for it," Black Sandra said with a giggle. "Two very good looking girls."

"Yeah, alright, don't rub it in."

"Well it looks like we both missed out," Black Sandra said as she gently placed her hand on Al's leg. "But... there will be other times and other adventures to be had."

"No, stop it," Al thought as images of him cavorting naked with Black Sandra, Fliss and Debs rushed to the front of his mind. *"I couldn't stand the pain of a hard-on right now."*

Black Sandra stayed for over an hour and left promptly when she caught sight of two police officers entering the hospital ward.

"Mr McIntosh," the officer said as he pulled out a wooden chair and sat by Al's side.

Al smiled.

"You, my son, are in a bad way."

Al recognised him as one of the police officers at the amusement arcade.

Al nodded.

"We know all about these black slags from Leicester," the officer continued. "Who the hell do they think they are trying to muscle in on London ground?"

Al winced as he tried to lift himself up.

"We want them and we want them bang to rights with the shooter!"

"I was mugged."

"Fuck off were you!"

"I was."

"Bollocks. It was that Leicester crew, wasn't it?"

"I didn't see anything."

"What the fuck are you playing at?"

Al took a sharp intake of breath as he tried to shrug his shoulders.

The officer was becoming visibly agitated.

"Someone has to do something about them and I need you to make a statement."

"I didn't see anything," Al said with a wince.

"I'm trying to help you and the people of Kings Cross," the officer said firmly. "Are you too stupid to see that?"

"If I could help you I would, but I was mugged from behind and didn't see anything."

"I wouldn't help you if I was at death's door and about to check out," Al thought. *"You lot will never understand the rules."*

The second officer closed his note pad and slid it into his jacket pocket.

"You're not doing us or yourself any favours" the first officer said as he rose sharply from the chair. "Come on, we've wasted enough time on this."

Al watched as both the police officers strutted down the ward and out into the hallway.

"I wouldn't tell you anything, ever!" Al thought as he allowed his head to rest deeper into the pillows.

Al thought about his life in Glasgow and how the bright lights of London had called him back. He remembered how Brian, his brother, had returned with Sandy, his girlfriend, on a motorbike and how they had included him in their registered mail scam. It had been so easy, the way they strolled in and picked up the mail bag and walked straight out of Kings Cross train station. He remembered how he felt when they opened the envelopes and placed the cash on the table in the squat that Mae West and Jean Harlow had found for him to stay in when he first visited London with nothing but a few pennies in his pocket.

"I still owe them," Al thought as he rested.

"Al, mate."

Al opened his eyes to see his friend Leaky and his brother Brian ambling through the ward towards him.

Al had befriended Leaky during their very first meeting. They occasionally did business together, but Leaky preferred fraud to violence. He had been born into money and his father had left him a significant sum, but the life of a criminal was what he aspired to. Leaky had been printing off fake five pound notes which he sold to the working girls in Kings Cross to hand back as change to their punters. He also moved large quantities of giros and family allowance books. In recent months he had moved into the fake passport and driving licence business.

Brian was a hard, dangerous man with a hair trigger temper. On one occasion Al had been in the pub, chatting with a number of new working girls, when one of the regulars sniffed his aftershave and said that he smelt like a poof. Al, knowing that it was just a harmless comment, laughed it off. However Brian took Al to one side and questioned why he allowed someone to speak to him that way. Brian was ready to inflict severe and savage punishment at a moment's notice.

Al tried for the third time without success, to sit more upright.

"Was it those bastards from Leicester?" Brian said as he pulled the chair towards him.

"Yeah," Al replied.

"How many?"

"I'm not sure; maybe eight, possibly ten," Al said. "They were all tooled up."

"They will need to pay for this," Brian said with a manic grin.

"They're probably long gone."

"If we find them, they're dead."

"You're lucky to be alive," Leaky said.

"That's thanks to Black Sandra."

"She's solid," Leaky said. "It didn't take long for this to get out."

"What do you mean?"

"Fucking Chinese whispers ain't it," Leaky said with a look of disgust. "This has grown arms and legs with rumours that your fighting days are over, you're in a wheelchair and no fucking good to anyone."

"That can be dangerous," Al muttered.

"Tell me about it," Leaky continued. "All your old enemies have already started crawling out of the woodwork."

"Fuck them!" Al growled. "Typical predatory behaviour; they think I'm done so they all want a piece of the action.

"I wouldn't worry about it," Brian said firmly.

"Nah, we'll hold everything at bay until you're out of here," Leaky said with a grin.

"Anyone steps out of place and they'll be dealt with," Brian said, clenching his fists.

"Anyway, on a lighter note," Leaky said with a chuckle. "Would you like us to get a couple of girls to visit to help make the time pass quicker?"

"Are you having a laugh?" Al winced. "I'm broken up, fractured and bruised from head to toe. At this moment in time I'm not even sure how I'm supposed to take a pee, let alone perform."

"Just a thought," Leaky said with a wink.

Al remained in the Royal Northern Hospital for two weeks before returning to Kings Cross.

Chapter 2

Al had been asking the working girls around the King Cross area if they had seen or heard anything about the Leicester gang. He concluded that after the shooting incident at the amusement arcade, they had packed up and returned to Leicester. Al was aware that his enemies had been sniffing around the many scams and money-making enterprises he had running, but his brother Brian and good friend Leaky made it abundantly clear that any move would result in violence.

"It feels good to be back outside and walking through Kings Cross," Al thought as he nodded to acknowledge two men talking by a Ford Capri. *"I missed this place even after just two weeks. There is no place on earth like Kings Cross at this moment in time."*

Al strolled down the street towards the Bell Pub. He stopped for a moment and inhaled deeply.

"Hmm, this London air just recharges you; physically, mentally and spiritually," Al thought before striding forward.

Al found that breathing in the cold London air replenished his body and had the powerful capability of keeping him alert to his environment and filling his mind with money making opportunities.

"Al, Al."

Al turned to see Betty Knocks racing towards him.

Betty Knocks was sixty years old but looked closer to eighty. She lived on the streets and would drink in the pubs around Kings Cross. She was disliked by a great number of people because of her raggedy clothes and poor hygiene. However, Al understood that she suffered with mental health issues and would, whenever he was in a pub where Betty was, order her a drink and stick it on his tab.

Al took a short step back as the musty odour of rotten eggs and cabbage assaulted his nasal passages.

"Fuck me Betty, you need a bath." Al thought, trying to avoid breathing in the putrid stench.

Betty took a deep draw on an Embassy cigarette butt she had found moments earlier and then casually dropped it to the ground.

"You owe me."

"What do you mean I owe you?"

Betty shook her head.

"Everyone knows it was you that turned over the taxi office where I sleep."

Betty slept in the doorway close to a taxi office. She considered that to be her area and should be paid a cut from any villainy that took place there.

"Not me," Al said firmly.

"Two thousand quid you got away with, and I want my cut," Betty persisted.

"You are not right in the head," Al thought.

"Keep your fucking voice down Betty," Al said with a glint of menace in his eyes. "Now listen and listen good. First and foremost that taxi rank job had fuck all to do with me, understand? Secondly, I never have and never will owe you fuck all for any business I carry out, are we clear?"

Al reached into his pocket and peeled off three ten pound notes.

"Get yourself over to Streatham Baths, clean yourself up, and then get yourself some new clobber from a charity shop."

Betty took the money.

"Then I want you to get yourself something decent and healthy to eat, okay?"

Betty nodded, still looking down at the three ten-pound notes.

Al turned swiftly on his heels and continued to walk towards the Bell pub.

"I fucking love this place," Al thought as he opened the door. *"Back where I belong."*

No sooner had Al stepped into the pub when there was a show of hands and acknowledgements from the locals. Al smiled and sauntered over to join Leaky and Brian while *'Don't You Want Me'* by The Human League played.

"Alright," Al said as he sat down. "Where's Sandy?"

Sandy was an enthusiastic biker and Brian's girlfriend.

"She's out on a bit of business," Brian said.

Al understood 'business' to be the picking up of a hessian post office bag full of registered letters from Kings Cross Station. He turned to see the barman place a pint of lager and a whiskey chaser on the table.

"Landlord says it's on the house and it's good to have you back."

"Cheers," Al said as he reached for the glass.

Al turned to the landlord, who was serving behind the bar, and raised his glass.

"Bootsie and Smudge were here a few days back; they send you their best," Leaky said before swallowing the last of his pint and raising his glass at the barman.

Leaky was supplying the South London duo with cheque books and most recently euro-cheque books. Each cheque book had twenty cheques that could be cashed for fifty pounds each.

"Good lads," Al said, remembering how the Millwall boys had laid into Newcastle United's 'Toon Army' when they descended on the pub.

"Business is still going good," Leaky said as his new pint was placed on the table.

"Is there anything I should know?"

Brian shook his head.

"A couple of chancers wandered into Large William's place while he was away, but we took care of them," Brian said with a grin.

Al had met Large William while serving time in Pentonville Prison. Large William had the most distinctive laugh and specialised in hijacking truckloads of cigarettes, booze and electrical equipment with a group of friends he'd known since school. He very quickly became a supplier for Al's spielers and in partial return, Al provided protection for Large William's pub.

"Any trouble in the pub?"

"No, we had a word with them outside."

"Good, cheers," Al said before scanning the bar.

Moments later Betty Knocks entered the pub as *'One of Us'* by Abba boomed out of the jukebox. Al shook his head.

"I told her to get herself cleaned up," Al thought, while humming the Abba tune to himself.

Betty caught Al's eye and traipsed over towards him like a movie extra from the George Romero 'Dawn of the Dead' zombie film.

"You owe me!" Betty said.

"Betty, we've just talked about this, remember?"

"Poor cow isn't all there," Al thought as motioned the barman to get Betty a drink.

"Fucking hell, Betty, you stink like rotting flesh!" Leaky said, covering his nose.

"There's a drink at the bar for you, now on your way," Al said calmly.

"You've got more patience than me," Leaky said as he sipped his lager.

Betty, without a word, traipsed over to the bar.

"She's not right," Al replied.

"Fucking nutcase and she smells foul," Leaky said, waving his hand frantically in front of his nose. "Betty smells worse than dog shit."

"I wouldn't give her the time of day," Brian said.

"If she asked me for money I'd back hand her," Leaky said as he leant back into his chair.

Al understood that people like Betty Knocks, with mental health issues, are easily overlooked and misunderstood. It wasn't as simple as 'pull yourself together' because the sufferer wasn't trying hard enough and just looking for a hand out or sympathy. Betty's failure to live a functional and happy life had nothing to do with the biological, psychological or sociological factors that society deemed living a normal life. Al's experience on the streets of Glasgow, at approved schools and in prison, taught him that mental health problems had nothing to with any lack of willpower as that alone was not enough, and getting the right treatment was extremely difficult.

"She's alright," Al said as a group of eight skinheads and two girls wearing Fred Perry Polo shirts entered the pub.

"Hello, this could be trouble," Brian said as he placed his lager on the beer mat.

All eight lads had shaved heads, wore tight blue jeans with high leg Doc Marten oxblood Boots, crisp, clean, and ironed Ben Sherman and Brutus shirts with button down collars and one quarter inch braces.

Al watched as they sauntered through the pub towards the bar.

Skinheads are a working class subculture that originated in London during the sixties and rapidly spread to all parts of the UK. Motivated by working class pride and solidarity, the movement gradually faded away to become replaced by Mod culture. In the late 1970s, the Rude Boy subculture re-emerged as Ska bands played the pubs and clubs before hitting the music charts.

"Ain't they supposed to be Nazis or something?" Leaky said as he watched the largest lad in his paisley Ben Sherman, order a round of drinks from the bar.

Al shook his head.

"I've seen them dancing about on Top of the Pops."

"They look a handful," Leaky said.

"Fuck them," Brian said as he shrugged his shoulders.

"There's a big difference between being tough and being dangerous," Al said.

"How do you mean?" Leaky asked.

"There were villains, well known villains and faces in the 1960s that people mistakenly believed to be hard bastards," Al said. "If a guy can have a stand-up row and go toe to toe with someone or a group of men with just his bare hands, then to me that makes him a hard bastard. However, if he waits until you've turned your back and comes at you with a tool or turns up mob handed to take down one fella on his own, then that's not a hard bastard, that's a dangerous man."

"That kinda makes sense," Leaky agreed. "I never really thought about it like that."

"There's a big difference."

"Either way someone is gonna get hurt though," Brian said.

"True but now take those lads over there," Al said as he nodded in their direction. "The shaven heads and boot boy look doesn't make them hard. It's what ticks between their ears and how far they are prepared to go."

"Violence is all part of our game but I don't particularly like it," Leaky said, slowly shaking his head. "I like the money, the women and the whole fuck-offness of being a villain."

Brian listened and then took a sip of his lager while Al and Leaky chuckled.

"Excuse me but are you Leaky?"

The three men looked up to see two young girls in their twenties.

"That would be me darling, how can I help you?"

Al knew immediately that the girls were on the game, but new to Kings Cross.

"I was told that you could help me with fivers," said the girl with the short blonde hair that shrouded her angular face.

"Who told you that?"

The girls looked at each other and then back at Leaky.

"Kate," the blonde whispered.

Leaky smiled.

"Did she tell you the price?"

The blonde relaxed, smiled, and then nodded.

Leaky reached into the sports bag he had under the table and handed the blonde a bundle of fivers.

"I can't take that many."

"You're new here?"

The two girls nodded.

"What are your names?"

"I'm Julie."

"And I'm Josey."

"Right, you can have these and pay me once you're on your feet, okay?"

"Thank you," Julie the blonde said as she pushed the fivers into her handbag.

"I'm Al," Al said as he stood up and shook both the girl's hands.

"We've heard about you."

Al smiled.

"All good I hope."

"Yeah, Kate said that you run things."

"I have a spieler, the American Bar; the place is full seven nights a week with rich punters looking for a drink, company and a good time."

"What's the catch?"

"There is no catch," Al said with a chuckle. "You party with the punters, get them to buy you drinks and there's a kick-back for you. Then anything you make for your time with them is all yours."

"Rich punters?"

"Seven nights a week," Al replied.

The two girls looked at each with broad smiles.

"We're in, thank you."

Al wrote down the address and handed it to Julie.

"Here," Leaky said as he handed Julie a second wad of fake fivers. "If you're working the American Bar, you'll need more of these."

"Thank you, thank you both," Josey said.

"No problem," Leaky said. "We're like one big dysfunctional family down here at Kings Cross."

"Oi, fuck face," the largest of the Skinheads called out. "This fucking lager's flat."

"No problem," the barman called back. "I'll get you a fresh pint."

"Alright," Wullie said as he sat down at Al's table.

Wullie was another of Al's brothers. He had arrived in London after taking time out from his job as a gamekeeper in Aberdeenshire. Al firmly believed that the reason his brother was so totally fucked up mentally was because of his vicious, brutal, psychotic excuse of a Mammy and abhorrent drunk of a father whose only care was for his precious Four Crown wine.

"I still haven't had words with you for what you did to my dog, Glen," Al thought as he watched Wullie take a sip from his drink. *"By rights I should batter you into next week."*

As much as Al would have wanted rightful retribution for what Wullie had done to his dog, he couldn't help balance the suffering that he had witnessed on both Wullie and his sister Beth. Mammy had hammered a sewing needle deep into Wullie's knee, while Beth would regularly be dragged screaming by her hair into the front room, stripped naked, and then beaten senseless with a dog chain.

"Calm down," Al thought as he visualised himself as a young boy playing his dog, Glen.

Al watched as the barman placed a new pint of lager in front of the Skinhead leader.

Al visualised his Mammy raising a clenched fist and then a second clutching a metal horseshoe.

"I fucking hate you mammy for all you did to us," Al thought as he watched the Skinhead leader take three huge gulps from the glass and then hand it back to the barmen.

"This pint is fucking flat too!"

"Yeah so is mine!" a second Skinhead yelled.

"Yeah and mine, you fucking Toby!"

Toby Jug was rhyming slang for mug... Toby Jug... Mug.

The two Skinhead girls looked uncomfortable.

The landlord looked over at Al.

Al was paid £200 weekly, on the books, as a bouncer for thirteen pubs in the Kings Cross Area. In addition he took ten percent from all villainy conducted within the pubs.

"Time to go to work," Al thought as *'Lip Up Fatty'* by Bad Manners played on the juke box.

The Skinheads were becoming rowdy.

"Come on, do your job and get us fresh drinks!"

"Yeah come on you ginger mug!"

"Chop, chop or you'll get a fucking slap!"

"I'm sorry, but you'll have to leave," the barman said awkwardly.

"Yeah, by you and whose army?" the Skinhead leader said as he stood up and shoved the barman's shoulder.

"Alright lads," Al said as he approached the table.

"What the fuck has it got to do with you?" the Skinhead leader growled through gritted teeth.

"I'll ask you nicely to just simmer down, lads, have a drink and enjoy your day out."

From the corner of his eye Al could see that Brian, Wullie, Leaky and two regulars were on their feet and edging towards the fracas.

"Who the fuck do you think you are?"

"I'm the guy that will decide if you leave here on your feet or get carried out on a stretcher," Al said as he lowered his tone.

"Fuck you!" the Skinhead leader yelled before firing a right hook that narrowly missed Al's head.

Al ducked backwards and then launched himself forward with a series of rapid left and right hooks. As each one connected, the Skinhead leader staggered back. The remaining Skinheads were on their feet. Al took a right hander to the side of the head before Brian punched the lad with such ferocity that he took off and landed across the table sending the lager glasses and their liquid contents smashing to the floor. Wullie had wrestled one Skinhead to the ground, clambered across his chest and with a firm grip of the lad's ears began smashing his head against the floor. Leaky took several aimless clumps before smashing a light ale bottle across one of the lad's heads. The Skinhead yelped in pain as blood from the side of his head spurted out and ran down his neck. The Skinhead leader tried to soak up the punches and fight back, but Al's reign of shots was powerful, targeted and relentless. Al held the Skinhead by the braces while he battered his face with one strike after another.

CRUNCH!

CRACK!

THUD!

The last of the Skinheads raised his hands in defeat as he saw his seven friends were battered, bruised and beaten.

"Alright, leave it out!"

Al let go of the Skinhead leader's braces and allowed his head to fall against the wooden floor.

"You picked the wrong place to cause trouble," Al said as he stepped closer to the last of the Skinheads. "All the pubs in Kings Cross are protected. If you foolishly decide to mob up and come back, I promise you this... some of you will not make your next birthday... do you understand me?"

"Gotcha," the Skinhead replied sheepishly.

"Right, you and your mates are out of here."

The Skinhead girls were off and out the door while the others were being helped back onto their feet by Brian, Leaky and few of the other lads. Al could see his brother, Wullie, just standing in the pub looking down at his bloody hands.

***

The following day Al had to go down to Kings Cross train station to collect a payment from some earlier business. On his return he saw one of the Skinhead girls from the previous day's skirmish walking towards him.

"Right, I'm in for a big mouthful here," Al thought as he came to a halt. *"Probably going to give it all the big one now about how we shouldn't have beaten up her troublemaker boyfriend."*

"It's you isn't it?"

"I am definitely me," Al said with a smile.

The Skinhead girl had shaven black hair with long bleach blonde fashioned into a Chelsea cut. She wore a black and gold Fred Perry polo shirt with a denim mini skirt made from a pair of Levi 501s, fishnet stockings and sexy white ankle socks with ox-blood brogue shoes.

Al couldn't help but notice that she had three gold studs in her right ear and wore black fingerless leather gloves on her hands.

"Loving those fishnets," Al thought.

"You set about my friends yesterday."

"What's your name?" Al asked bluntly.

"Ella, my friends call me Ella."

"Listen Ella, I'm Al, and your friends just kicked off in the wrong place, that's all."

"Tell me about it!"

Al was a little taken back.

"Ray is a fucking nightmare!"

"Ray?"

"Yeah, he likes to call himself Reaper, but we all know he's Ray and ever since Sham 69 released *'If the Kids are United'* he has set himself up as some kind of Skinhead leader."

"So what is he, your boyfriend or something?"

Ella looked into Al's eyes and smiled.

"Do you fancy a cup of tea?"

"Sure," Al said as he momentarily glanced down at her fishnet stockings.

Ella giggled and then led the way to a café. Once inside the café Al bought two teas and two bacon sandwiches.

"You didn't have to buy these," Ella said before taking a bite from the sandwich.

"My pleasure," Al replied while taking a small sip from his boiling hot tea.

"So, Ray is your boyfriend?"

"Yeah, and he's a fucking idiot!"

"Why is that?"

"He thinks that he is some kind of tough nut and other Skinheads just gravitate towards him, which only fuels his monster ego more."

"So why are you with him?"

Ella shook her head.

"He wasn't always like this, Al."

Al popped the last of his sandwich into his mouth.

"When we first got together, he was charming, attractive, intelligent, kind, and funny."

Ella chuckled for a few seconds.

"I truly believed that I had found the perfect guy for me," Ella said. "Then, bit by bit he changed. He became overly attentive and helpful. It was like he just wanted whatever was best for me. Ray would have everyone believe that he's a strong, hard, nut, who knows what he wants, and only says something if he means it. It's only in recent months that I've seen this charm evolve into some kind of manipulation."

"I wonder if they're stockings or tights," Al thought as he sipped his tea.

"It's like him being nice to me is dependent on me going along with whatever he wants."

"That sounds a bit controlling to me," Al said.

"Yeah, he thinks because his silly Skinhead mates do what he says, that I should jump without question too," Ella said, before wiping the brown sauce from her lips. "If I don't then he'll cop the hump and not call for days, or blank me when we're out. He's even taken the piss out of me once or twice to make me look small."

"That's not nice."

"He seems to think that I just have to agree with his opinions even if I think he's well out of order," Ella said. "There was a bunch of us that wanted to go and see Adam and the Ants last year at the Marquis. This was before they had records in the charts. Everyone was talking about their gigs and how much energy they put into their live shows. Anyway, Ray pulls a mob of Skins together and off we go. I had asked for just a few of us to go so we could really enjoy the show without any grief or aggro, but oh no, Ray wanted to go mob handed."

"Adam and the Ants; that's the pirate looking bloke isn't it?" Al thought as he listened intently.

"Most of the people in the Marquis were just music lovers looking for a good night out, but when whoever it was that plays the background music put on Sham 69 that was it. I mean Ray and his mates just went fucking mental; jumping around and clumping anyone and everyone in sight. He totally fucked up a great night out

35

and when I said so he got the right hump with me," Ella said. "I actually found myself holding back my opinions in case it set him off."

"No one should ever stop you having a voice."

"Fucking right," Ella said with a grin. "Ray has been treating me like one of his gang who has to do what he says."

"He sounds like the kind of bloke who likes to exert his dominance at all costs."

"He does," Ella said. "This isn't the same Ray that I first started going out with."

Al looked down into his empty mug of tea.

"The changes have been so gradual and controlled, it's almost shocking sometimes when I think of how he changed from this kind, charming, fun, guy to a fucking animal that insists everything goes his way. If I want to do something and he doesn't, then it's just too fucking bad for me."

Al shook his head.

"I hardly know this girl," Al thought as he caught another glimpse of her fishnet stockings. *"She can do better than this mug, Ray, though."*

"Do you know that yesterday I actually called him to let him know what I was wearing to the pub?"

"Really?"

"My friend, Donna, warned me off Ray about a year ago and to this day I still don't know how Ray managed to turn me against her,"

Ella muttered. "I dropped her, ignored her calls and blanked her on nights out and all because Ray had put this huge, invisible, wedge between us."

"I'm glad I smashed the fucker's face in," Al thought as he watched Ella become visibly upset.

"He sounds like a bully boy that wants you to rely on him and him alone," Al said.

"He is."

Ella sighed heavily.

"He's manipulating you to get what he wants so you feel like you're back in his good books."

"That's exactly what he does."

"Does he ask where you've been or who you've been with?"

Ella nodded.

"Other than Julie, I don't have any girlfriends these days, and I dare not stop and chat with a friend from school."

"Why?"

"I bumped into a couple of lads from my school at a pub with Julie. There no history between any of us. We were all just friends that hung around by the bike sheds during lunchtimes sharing cigarettes and having a good laugh. Like I said, I have never been out with either of these lads. Anyway, when Ray asked me where I had been, I innocently said that we had a few drinks with these friends from school and he went berserk. He wanted to know what pub they drank in, where they worked and where they lived. Ray was talking about taking the Skins down to the pub to smash it up and kick the fuck out these two lads for just having a harmless drink with old friends."

"I've seen this kind of behaviour before," Al thought. *"It never ends well."*

"Did he find them?"

"Yeah but not straight away; it must have been a couple of months later. We had been out on the lash and stopped off for a bag of chips after the pub closed, and the two lads were in there waiting when Julie has just said hi. Of course they turned around and started talking. I was shitting myself. I could see Ray was becoming agitated. I just kept it to a weak smile and answered yes and no. The last thing I wanted was for Ray to stir up the lads and give my friends a good kicking."

"He's a nasty piece of work and you could do better."

Ella paused for moment and then smiled.

"I'm pleased that you gave him and his silly mates a good hiding."

"He tried his luck in the wrong place."

"Ray has become dark and nasty and I don't need that kind of shit in my life."

"You're an attractive girl, Ella. A good relationship is built on trust, loyalty, and mutual respect."

"You're right," Ella said.

Ella looked deep into Al's eyes and began to smile.

"What?" Al said with a chuckle.

"Do you have a girlfriend?"

"I am very definitely not good boyfriend material," Al said with a raucous laugh. "My relationships rarely last more than a single night and in my line of work it suits me."

"Al."

"Yeah."

"Would you like to fuck me?"

Once the initial shock settled, Al's mouth broadened into a smile.

"I would love to fuck you, Ella, but with no strings."

Ella rose from her chair.

"Do you have a place nearby?"

"There's a hotel around the corner."

"Perfect."

Al led Ella through Kings Cross Station to the taxi rank outside. He opened the door to a black London Taxi.

"Hello mate, The Morton Hotel in Woburn Place," Al said as he closed the taxi door and sat next to Ella.

"Hmm, you smell delicious," Al thought as their legs touched.

"You're not a wham bam thank you ma'am kind of guy are you, Al?" Ella whispered.

"Definitely not."

Al closed his eyes as the tingles raced through his body.

"It's refreshing to be with a woman who knows what she wants," Al whispered.

"I fucking hope they're stockings." Al thought as he gently squeezed her thigh.

"Ray would shy off from conversations about sexual needs and desires," Ella whispered. "It was his loss because we never progressed beyond keeping his ego in check."

"This could be the fuck of the century," Al thought as the taxi came to a halt outside the Morton Hotel.

"There you go mate," Al said as he handed the taxi driver his fare.

As they stood on the pavement looking up at the hotel sign, Al turned to Ella.

"Is there anything else you would like to do?"

Ella smiled like a vixen on heat.

Al paid for the room and led Ella towards the lift. Once they were on the second floor, Al checked his key number, and took Ella by the hand. He opened the door and was pleasantly surprised by how nice the room had been decorated.

Chapter 3

Al had spent the day, that night and most of the following day at the Morton hotel with Ella. He walked her back to Kings Cross Station after they shared a late lunch together. There was no talk of meeting again. Ella kissed Al on the cheek before trotting off towards the barriers that led out to the train platform.

Al called into each of his spielers to collect the night's takings.

"Business is good, bloody good!" Al thought as he patted his pocket. *"I think I'll stop by the Scottish Stores for a couple."*

As Al strode along the Caledonian Road, he spotted a conman known as 'Pilot' taking short sips from a bottle of wine and tugging hard on a cigarette. Al knew him to dress up in Army or Navy uniforms to carry out his cons. On one occasion Pilot had dressed up as a priest in his full regalia.

"I'm going to make a point of getting to know Pilot," Al thought. *"I'd like him to work for me. I reckon we could make some serious money."*

With an image in his head of Pilot dressed up as a priest, he remembered being on remand in Brixton when a priest had told him how women were no good whores, especially those locked away in Holloway Prison. He went on to describe how they would file into his confession box and tell him how they had been dreaming of their boyfriend's cock deep inside them before asking for forgiveness. The priest believed, passionately, that all women were pond life, scum and the scourge of mankind. Al's cell mate,

Billy, later confided in him that the priest would trade a bottle of vodka in return for being fucked in the confession box.

"Hypocrites, the lot of them," Al thought as he continued towards the pub.

"Get your tits out

Get your tits out

Get your tits out for the boys

Get your tits out for the boys!"

"What's going on here?" Al thought as he approached a group of men in a circle singing at the top of their voices near the Scottish Stores pub.

Through a small gap he saw that it was Betty Knocks dancing naked around her pile of scruffy clothes.

"She needs proper help," Al thought as he entered the pub.

Instantly Al spotted two mean characters that he hadn't seen in the pub before.

"They don't look like punters up here for the girls," Al thought as he strode over to the bar.

"Usual Al?"

"Yeah, cheers."

Moments later a pint of lager with a whiskey chaser was placed in front of him.

Al raised the whiskey glass and swallowed it in one before taking a long sip from the ice-cold glass of lager.

"Al, mate."

Al turned to see Dublin Dave, a regular in the pub, who engaged in a wide range of villainy and never failed to pay Al what was due.

"Alright Dave."

"Yeah, I've brought a couple of mates with me," Dublin Dave said, pointing over at the two men Al had spotted on his way in.

"Okay."

"I know them and we've done business for years."

Al took a long sip of his lager.

"The big six foot four fella on the right is Big Dibs and the other one is Ginger Jim."

"Dublin lads?" Al asked.

"Yeah, both good lads and I can vouch for them."

Al smiled.

"That's good enough for me, have a good night."

"Cheers Al."

Al scanned the pub. His eyes fell on three new girls he hadn't seen before, and concluded that they must have been new to Kings Cross. Behind them sat Monty.

"I just don't get what makes that bloke tick," Al thought as he motioned the barman to refill his glass.

Monty was a hard, dangerous man from Belfast who hated Al with a vengeance. It began when he first started dating one of the working girls, Michelle, from Leeds. During their talks after sex, she confessed to having slept with Al some months earlier. Monty dumped her immediately and then took up with another working girl, Deneen, from Hull. They were together only a short time before she, too, having been badgered by Monty, said that she had a one night fling with Al almost two years before meeting him. Monty was in a fit of rage and confronted Al who calmly explained that she had been a one night stand years before she had even met him. They agreed to disagree, so Monty decided to drown his sorrows with neat whiskey. Within a few hours he was drunk. He clambered up onto the bar in the Duke of Edinburgh pub, undid his trousers and waved his cock around screaming 'This is what that bastard Al has been giving my girlfriends'. Al confronted him and expected a violent reaction. He was surprised when Monty apologised to both Al and to everyone in the pub before leaving. Months later Monty met and fell in love with Patsy from Bristol. They made an odd couple but Monty was besotted with her and asked her to marry him. Patsy was a stunning looking girl and was ready to settle down, so she agreed, and the two of them had a quiet wedding followed by an old-fashioned booze up at the Scottish Stores. Monty was drunk when he left to start their honeymoon at a pre-booked hotel in the West End. It transpired that Monty, in a drunken, jealous, state, began questioning Patsy about her previous lovers. When she confessed to sleeping with Al he became enraged. Monty saw red and in a blind rage took a lighter out of his jacket pocket and proceeded to torture her by burning her ears. Patsy was rushed to hospital with multiple burns, while Monty slipped away into the night. Patsy from Bristol was mentally scarred for life because of a liaison that happened long before Monty had come onto the scene.

Monty hated Al.

Al had been right to be cautious of Monty because he was unpredictable. Al was told how Monty had been barked at by one of two German shepherd dogs. Monty punched and kicked one of the dogs before ramming a screwdriver through the dog's skull. The second dog, having witnessed the horrific killing ran off into the night howling at the top of its voice and was never seen again. The Judge gave Monty four years.

With *'Babooshka'* by Kate Bush playing in the background, the door to the pub swung open and in pranced Betty Knocks, stark naked.

A few of the locals cheered while others called for her to get dressed. Betty began to gyrate her old and wrinkled body seductively and moved towards the table where Dublin Dave was sitting with his two friends Big Dibs and Ginger Jim.

Al could see that none of them were impressed or in the least bit entertained by her antics. Betty launched herself towards Ginger Jim.

"Fuck off you old crone!"

Betty Knocks, undeterred, launched herself towards him again. Ginger Jim shoved her away. As Betty stumbled backwards and fell to the floor, Monty was up and out of his seat and racing across the bar towards Ginger Jim. He grabbed a handful of Ginger Jim's hair then took out a sharpened barber's razor and sliced it across his throat. Blood immediately spurted out onto Ginger Jim's clothing and the table. Monty calmly put the razor into his pocket and returned to his table to finish his drink.

The ambulance was called. It arrived in minutes along with two squad cars and uniformed police officers. Ginger Jim was treated by the paramedics before being taken to hospital.

Monty had slipped away but someone had put his name in the frame.

The officers asked around the pub where they could find Monty.

"Lads, can I have a word?"

Al went outside with one of the police officers.

"Look this should never have happened," Al said.

"Yeah, so what are you saying?" the officer replied.

"Oh, you know what's coming," Al thought as he reached into his pocket.

"I've got five thousand quid here if you lads just fill in the paperwork and turn a blind eye."

The officer rubbed his chin before standing upright.

"Ten grand and its gone."

"Done," Al said as he shook the bent copper's hand. "I'll give you this five grand now and the balance in a couple of days."

"I can do that," the copper said.

The police made themselves scarce. Dublin Dave was embarrassed and apologised for Ginger Jim's behaviour before leaving for the hospital with Big Dibs. Al made it known to the faces that the old bill had been bought for ten grand and he had already stumped up five of it. Within minutes a whip round produced just over four and a half grand. Al was happy to make up the balance.

Even though Al knew that Monty hated him with a vengeance, he also knew that if it were to ever go off in a pub, then Monty, despite their differences, would fight any outsider shoulder to shoulder with Al. For that reason Al paid off the corrupt old bill.

***

The officer arrived back at the Scottish Stores pub the following evening and took the outstanding five thousand pounds from Al before driving off with his colleague, to arrest Monty. Al was told that the two corrupt officers had used the ten thousand pounds to pay for a holiday in New York. Monty was charged and sentenced to eight years. He blamed Al for the arrest, claiming that he had been set up. Everyone who knew Monty told him that Al had been the one rallying to his rescue, but he wouldn't have it. He vowed that he would kill Al McIntosh at the very first opportunity he got.

Chapter 4

Al stopped by Limerick Mick's arcade where the final battle had taken place with the Leicester mob.

"I heard about Monty," Limerick Mick said as they walked through the busy arcade.

"Yeah, nasty business," Al replied as he looked down at the Space Invaders machine.

'Another One Bites The Dust' by Queen played through the speaker system.

"Everyone has told him that it was you who put up the money to get him off, but he just wasn't having any of it."

"It'll be what it'll be then," Al said calmly.

"I'm still looking for protection for this place if you're interested," Limerick Mick said, shrugging his shoulders.

Al looked around at the pinball machines, crane and claw, slots and the coin operated games.

"No problem," Al said. "It'll be two hundred quid a week and you put me on the books as a bouncer, alright?"

"It's better to be safe than sorry," Limerick Mick said as he watched several men feeding the slot machines. "I have a good business and I need it to stay that way."

"I'll drop by from time to time just to check things out," Al said. "If it looks like it could get nasty then call the Bell pub and word will be with me in no time and it'll be sorted."

"Great, I appreciate it," Limerick Mick said as he shook Al by the hand.

Al took one last look at the brightly lit, flashing lights before turning swiftly on his heels and leaving.

"Another one gone and another one gone, another one bites the dust" Al sang to himself as he strolled towards the Scottish Stores pub.

As Al opened the pub doors he immediately spotted Jackie O'Docherty drinking a pint and surrounded by several regulars.

Jackie O'Docherty was a big name in protection and a good friend of Dougie 'The Man' McKinnon who previously ran Kings Cross like a 1960s sixties gangster with his side-kick and one-time armed robber, 'Heart Attack'. Al had very quickly seen through their flimsy empire and concluded that Dougie 'The Man' McKinnon's days were numbered.

Jackie's large, bulbous, nose was crooked and hung over his fat upper lip. His almond brown eyes were like slits and looked too close together. Jackie's complexion was dark and covered in scars from a lifetime of violent confrontations.

"Well fuck me," Jackie said, getting to his feet. "It's good to see you Al."

"How are you?" Al asked as he shook Jackie's hand.

"Just happy to be out," Jackie said before sitting back in his seat.

Jackie O'Docherty had been arrested and convicted for Grievous Bodily Harm. He was weighed off for three years.

Al motioned the barman to bring over a round of drinks.

"So what are you doing back here?" Al asked, keeping his eyes firmly fixed on Jackie's.

"I'm not here looking for trouble if that's what you mean," Jackie said with a smile before sipping his pint. "I'm on the out and just wanted to party with some old friends."

The barman placed a tray of drinks on the table.

"Cheers Al," Jackie said as he raised his glass. "It's good to be back on the manor with friends again."

"What is this fucker up to?" Al thought as he sat down opposite him.

"Somebody put some music on," Jackie called out. "This is a party."

Moments later *'Going Back to My Roots'* by Odyssey began to play.

"How appropriate is this?" Jackie called out before taking several large sips from his glass.

The tension in the pub died away as the drinks flowed towards the table where Al, Jackie and several of the regulars sat.

"I bumped into Monty while at the Ville," Jackie said.

Al and the regulars understood the Ville to mean HMP Pentonville Prison.

"He holds you responsible for him being banged up," Jackie said as he placed his drink on the table.

"That's bollocks," one of the regulars said.

"Yeah, it was Al that got everyone to chip in and pay off the old bill," said another. "Monty has it all wrong."

"I'm just telling you as a mate, Al, because he's going around telling everyone that you're fucking dead when he gets out," Jackie said.

"I'll sort it one way or another when the time is right," Al said, fixing his gaze firmly on Jackie.

"I just thought you'd need to know because he's a dangerous fucker."

Al understood that there was a big difference between being a hard man and dangerous man. A hard man will go toe to toe with his fists, while a dangerous man will wait until your back is turned and then use a tool.

Al smiled and shrugged his shoulders.

"You are one cool cookie," Jackie said. "It's good to see you again."

"I don't trust a word that leaves those fat lips," Al thought.

After five pints Jackie let out a loud and long raucous belch.

"Do you know what I could do with now?" Jackie said as he patted his stomach. "Something good to eat and then a couple of hours romping about with a brass."

"There's a good Chinese around the corner," Al said as he rose from his chair.

"Yeah, I know it," Jackie said. "Good grub if I remember it right."

Al, Jackie and three of the regulars, Sid, Ron and Tom, left the pub and ambled down to the Chinese Restaurant in Pancras Square. Sid opened the door and the lads all filed in.

"Alright," Al said to the young Asian waitress with a smile. "Can we have a table for five please?"

The pretty young waitress smiled and showed them through the restaurant, past a large freestanding gold dragon ornament, to a round table covered in a white table cloth. The walls were decorated in a deep crimson red with a myriad of red and gold paintings of dragons.

The five men sat down and then immediately ordered five pints of lager. Al was wearing his new full length leather trench coat and placed it over the back of his chair.

"This is on me," Al said as he browsed through the menu. "So, order whatever you fancy."

"Cheers Al."

"Yeah, thanks."

"Nice one."

"Much appreciated Al," Jackie said before placing the menu on the table.

"Can I take your order?" the pretty young waitress asked.

The lads ordered a mix of special fried rice, Singapore noodles, sweet and sour chicken, pork balls, crispy duck and a chicken curry.

"I'd like her to slip under this table and sort this out," Jackie whispered, grabbing his crotch.

"There's a hundred and one brasses back at Kings Cross that will happily take care of that for you," Al replied.

Just as Jackie finished his pint, the food arrived.

"That was quick," Al thought as he smiled and sat back in his seat.

Al watched as the restaurant began to fill up with tourists and businessmen.

"What the fuck is this?" Jackie yelled out before spitting a mouthful of rice out onto his plate. "Oi, you!"

The young waitress hurried over to the table.

"What is the problem, sir?"

"Have this!" Jackie shouted before flicking a forkful of rice at the girl. "It ain't bloody cooked!"

Al was shocked by Jackie's behaviour.

"Alright, leave it out," Al said firmly.

Undeterred, Jackie grabbed a handful of the rice and threw it at the young girl.

"I've had better rice in the nick!"

The stunned young waitress ran off towards the kitchen. Moments later three older Chinese women kicked the kitchen door open and raced towards the table brandishing meat cleavers.

"What the fuck?" Al said as he rose quickly to his feet.

He grabbed his chair and raised it up in front of him just as one of the women took a swing with the cleaver. She took the bottom of the wooden leg clean off.

"Let's have it!" Jackie shouted before grabbing the table and turning it over. The food and cutlery crashed and splattered on the black and white chequered flooring.

A massive fourth woman who looked like she had been eating a Chinese restaurant a day since birth, appeared from nowhere and took an almighty swing at Jackie.

SMACK!

Her fist connected with Jackie's jaw. His legs collapsed from under him and he fell onto the floor, unconscious.

Sid, Ron and Tom managed to avoid the wild slashing and stabbing from the irate workers.

"Calm down!" Al yelled, trying to put his leather trench coat on.

The four older Chinese workers had hate in their eyes and wanted blood for what Jackie had done.

"It's the old bill!" Sid said before racing off towards the door.

Al could hear the police sirens getting louder.

"I better get out of here," Al thought as stepped out from behind the table.

His attacker clambered over the damaged chair and took another swing at Al with her meat cleaver.

"*Missed!*" Al thought as he followed Ron and Tom out of the door and into the street.

Jackie had been knocked out and was still in the restaurant.

Sid, Tom and Ron scrambled off down an alleyway while Al stomped back towards the Scottish Stores pub.

"*What the fuck was that all about?*" Al thought. "*She was just a young girl! What the hell was that mug, Jackie, thinking?*"

Once back inside the pub, Al took off his new black leather trench coat.

"*What the...?*" Al thought when he spotted a cut in the coat that started by the collar and ran right down to the waist. "*I paid two hundred and fifty quid for this!*"

Al ordered a whiskey and sat down at his usual table.

"*That was bloody stupid,*" Al thought as he reached for his glass. "*That's a local for me. I like the people and the food is bloody good.*"

Al took a small sip of his drink.

"*Jackie was well and truly out of order, but that said, I'll need to try and get the charges dropped against him,*" Al thought before knocking back the double whiskey.

Al used the pub's phone and called the Chinese restaurant. He asked to speak with the manager. Al explained that Jackie had been rude and was out of order. After Al promised to pay for everything, the manager agreed to work with him.

***

Jackie was arrested and held in the police cells overnight and then taken to the magistrate's court the following morning. As agreed between the restaurant's manager and Al, none of the staff turned up to give evidence against Jackie, so the charges were dropped. Al was waiting outside the court when a uniformed police sergeant approached him.

"I know you," the police sergeant said. "I know your type."

"Sorry but I've never laid eyes on you before," Al replied calmly.

"You hurt one of my young officers, Al McIntosh."

"I don't have a clue what you're talking about."

"We arrested Kevin Summers with twenty thousand train tickets and we know it was you that sold them."

"Your lot put me in front an ID parade and I wasn't identified," Al said firmly. "It wasn't me."

"We know it was you and we will get you!" the police sergeant hissed.

"Really," Al said as he squared up to the sergeant. "So why don't you just fit me up like every other fucking old bill does."

The police sergeant smiled and shook his head.

"If I can't get you the right way then I won't, but mark my words, Al McIntosh, one of these days I will get you bang to rights and when you're standing in front of a judge and being sent down for a long time, you'll look over and see me standing right there seeing justice done."

"An honest copper...I'm shocked!" Al thought.

The police sergeant looked Al up and down and then bounded up the steps towards the court house.

As the police sergeant entered the court Al spotted Jackie O'Docherty stepping out.

Al raised his hand.

Jackie walked gingerly down to Al.

"Al, I don't what to say, mate. I'm so embarrassed."

"So you should be!"

"I am sorry mate. I haven't had a drink in a while and it was just too much too soon."

"Right, what are your plans?"

"Plans?"

"Don't be coy, Jackie, I want to know what your plans are."

"I thought I'd hang around the Cross and make a few quid."

Al took a step closer to Jackie.

"Let's get this fucking right, Jackie, because I will only tell you once," Al said as he leaned in towards Jackie. "Everything in Kings Cross has changed, and you and yesterday's crew are all over. You may be a well-known face, but you will not be walking back into any of your old rackets because they're mine and the Combination's."

The Combination was a name that Al, Brian, Leaky and his crew had been named by a rival gang led by Dougie 'The Man' McInnon, because they stuck together.

"You will have to find your own earners."

"Okay," Jackie said sheepishly.

"We will help you when it's needed, but make no mistake, we run Kings Cross. Am I making myself clear?"

"Crystal clear, Al."

"What are up to now?"

"I was going to get a drink at the Scottish Stores and then get a brass."

"Are you alright for money?" Al said, reaching into his pocket.

"I'm fine... but thanks."

Al left Jackie to contemplate his future and the rules of operating in Kings Cross. After doing his rounds and spending an adventurous afternoon with Black Sandra and her friend, he returned to the Scottish Stores to have a pint with Leaky and Brian. He found Jackie drunk and asleep at the bar. He had wrapped his arm around the inside of the wrought iron shelves above the counter.

"I'll need to a keep an eye on Jackie O'Docherty," Al thought as he sat down with Leaky and Brian. *"This guy is going to be trouble."*

Chapter 5

Al's brother, Brian and his girlfriend had been strolling into Kings Cross station and leaving with a sack full of registered letters that were almost always stuffed with cash. The scam had been netting them an average of three thousand pounds most weeks. It had been Sandy that introduced Brian to the business when they were first together in Glasgow.

They had planned to go down to Kings Cross on the Friday morning, but Brian had to help Al with some work at one of his spielers that morning. Sandy was supposed to wait for Brian to return but instead she strolled off down to the station to lift the bags on her own, just as she had scores of times before. Sandy arrived at Kings Cross Station and casually sauntered in and made her way to where the post office sacks were generally left on the platform. As always, she looked to her left and then right before picking up the sack containing the registered letters. She taken less than five steps when several plain clothes and uniformed officers sprang out of their hiding places and arrested her. Sandy dropped the bag and held her hands above her head. She was handcuffed and frogmarched out of the station and thrown into the back of a waiting police van. Once inside the police station, they tried to get her to grass on her accomplice, Brian, but despite their offers to go easy on her, she stuck rigid and owned up to it all. Sandy was remanded in HMP Holloway without bail.

"I'm sorry to hear about Sandy," Leaky said as he sat down at their usual table.

"Cheers," Brian said before motioning the barman to bring over a round of drinks.

"That is what you call staunch," Leaky said as he pulled his chair in closer to the table. "Nicked and never said a word...what a girl!"

"She certainly is," Brian said.

"I suppose that bit of business has dried up now?"

"I did take a walk down to Kings Cross Station yesterday," Brian said. "There was a guard standing by the post office sacks. Unless you give him a slap and have it on your toes then it's as good as dead now."

"All good things inevitably come to an end," Leaky said.

"Not necessarily," Al said with a grin. "There is always another bit of business just waiting to be discovered. That's what I love about London and Kings Cross."

Just as *'All Over the World'* by the Electric Light Orchestra boomed out of the pub's speakers, the pub door opened and a young man with short cropped brown hair, blue jeans, trainers and a Fred Perry polo shirt looked around the pub.

"Al... Brian!" the young man called out enthusiastically.

"It's John," Brian said.

Al looked over to see his younger brother John. He rose from his chair and beckoned him over.

"John, what are you doing here?"

Al hadn't seen his brother John in over five years.

"I'm done with Glasgow," John said as he shook Al's and then his brother Brian's hand. "I thought I'd try my luck down here in London."

"John, this is my good friend Leaky."

Leaky shook John's hand firmly.

Al motioned the barman over.

"What are you drinking?"

John looked down at the table that was littered with empty glasses.

"I'll have whatever it is you guys are having."

Al ordered another round of lager with whiskey chasers.

"So what did you do in Glasgow?" Leaky said. "What was your business?"

"I did a bit of painting and decorating with a local building firm," John said as he sat down. "It was alright but the private jobs paid better."

"So you're looking to pick up a bit of work down here," Leaky said before winking at Al.

"I'm open to everything," John said before looking around the pub. "This is London, the capital of the world... right?"

The barman cleared away the empty glasses before putting the fresh tray of drinks down.

John told Al, Brian and Leaky how he had become bored with working the nine to five and paying a big chunk of his pay check to the taxman. He was looking for adventure and was sure that if his brothers, Al and Brian, were in London, there must be a pound note and plenty of fun to be had.

John had drunk the last of his second pint when he looked over at three girls at the bar wearing high heels and short skirts.

"Have you seen those girls at the bar?"

Leaky chuckled.

"Kings Cross is full of them," Leaky said. "You wait until tonight, this place and every other pub around here will be packed with pretty good time girls."

John turned back to the girls and smiled.

"She smiled back," John whispered.

"Really," Leaky said with a chuckle.

"Yeah, they all did."

"You could be in there," Leaky said before sinking the last of his whiskey.

"You reckon?"

"I'm certain of it."

"What do you think Al?"

"John, this isn't like anything in Glasgow, or anywhere else in the country come to that."

"How do you mean?" John said as he shuffled his chair closer to the table.

"Those girls and hundreds more just like them are all available but... at a price."

"A price?" John repeated with a quizzical expression.

"They're brasses," Leaky said.

"Brasses?"

"Working girls, John," Al said with a smile.

"Working girls?"

"Oh for fuck's sake, John," Brian said finally. "They're prostitutes, on the game, brasses. They will fuck you and anyone else for money."

"You're joking!"

Al, Brian and Leaky all shook their heads.

"So you don't have to take them out to the cinema, buy them drinks and then hope to get a feel?"

"No," Brian said. "You agree a price and you'll get to do pretty much whatever you like."

"Provided it's all agreed beforehand," Al said.

"It gets better," Leaky said with a mischievous grin. "Some of them will work together. You pay a bit more but you'll get twice the fun."

"He's kidding, right?"

Al and Brian both shook their heads.

The pub door opened just as *'Give Me the Night'* by George Benson played, and in strutted four shapely girls in high heel shoes and short skirts.

"No wonder you two are down here," John said as he watched the girls strut across the bar and join the other girls. "This place is heaven."

"Actually John," Al said with a serious expression. "This can also be an extremely dangerous place, so you must keep your wits about you and treat everyone as you would expect to be treated yourself."

"Yeah of course," John said, watching the girls at the bar.

"How much money do you have on you?" Al said as he reached into his trouser pocket and pulled out a large wad of notes.

"Bloody hell!" John said when he spotted the cash. "I've got about thirty five pounds."

Al proceeded to flick through the wad of ten and twenty pound notes before peeling off two hundred pounds and handing it to John.

John looked down at the cash and then back at Al.

"Thank you."

"It'll cost you about fifteen quid for a shag," Leaky said. "That is unless you want something a bit kinky. Just make sure that you give them the right money because you won't want one of my fivers in your change."

"Your fivers?"

"That's a story for another time," Al said. "Why don't you get yourself over to the bar and get yourself sorted. Tell them that we're brothers and you'll be looked after."

"Are you sure you don't mind?" John said before smiling at a shapely girl with long tresses of ash blonde hair that swooped over her shoulders and shrouded her pretty face.

"Knock yourself out," Leaky said with a chuckle. "You're in Kings Cross."

"Once you're done, make your way back here and we'll sort you somewhere to stay."

"Thanks Al and Brian, and it's good to meet you Leaky," John said before getting up.

Al grinned to himself as he watched his younger brother, John, amble over to the girls.

"We'll need to keep an eye on him," Brian said.

Al and Leaky agreed.

"Have you heard about Jackie O'Docherty?"

"What the fuck has he been up to now?" Al thought.

"I'm being told that he's making out that he's on the firm, one of the Combination."

"I never did like that ugly bastard," Brian said.

"Well he is certainly ugly," Leaky said with a raucous laugh.

"What's been happening?" Al said with a sigh.

"His antics are bringing attention to us, Al."

"I'll have a word," Al said.

"I'll fucking have a word with him if you like," Brian said, clenching and unclenching his fists.

"Leave it with me," Al said firmly.

"Well, speak of the devil," Leaky said, just as Jackie O'Docherty strode into the pub with a stunning redhead on his arm.

"Hello Al, Brian, Leaky. This is Margaret," Jackie said as he approached their table.

Margaret had rouge-red hair that spiralled and tumbled over her shoulders. Her eyes were an alluring jade-green while her puffy lips were kiss-inspiring and satin soft.

"What a stunner," Al thought as he casually looked her up and down.

"We were just talking about you," Brian said.

Al immediately shot him a look and shook his head.

"It's nice to meet you, Margaret," Al said.

"Likewise," Leaky said.

Brian smiled briefly and took a sip from his drink.

"It's nice to meet you too," Margaret said with a grin. "I've heard so much about you."

"All good, I hope," Al replied. "Would you like a drink?"

Margaret asked for a gin and tonic while Jackie took two chairs from the adjoining table.

"Don't mind if we join you, do you?"

Jackie proceeded to tell them how he and Margaret had met.

"I was at that strip joint in Bourchier Street, Soho, when Margaret strutted out on stage in the skimpiest of outfits. Lads, I could not take my eyes off her and I could tell that she liked me too."

"You're an ugly bastard Jackie... she likes the colour of your money and that's about it," Al thought.

"I caught her eye, and when she smiled back, I just knew that it was something special, know what I mean?"

Al and Leaky reluctantly nodded.

"There was something just so powerful and sexy about him, so I asked him back to my place after the show," Margaret said. "Basically, he never left and we've been together ever since."

"Well I'm pleased for you both," Al said.

"Can I get you boys a drink?" Jackie said.

"Cheers," Leaky said as he raised his empty glass.

"I bet Jackie was a good tipper," Leaky said.

"Oh yes, he's very generous," Margaret said.

"He would need to be to share your bed every night," Al thought.

"Don't you just love Abba?" Margaret said as *'Dancing Queen'* by Abba played on the juke box. "I do a routine at the club to Money, Money, Money. You should come over and catch it some time."

"She's hitting on me," Al thought. *"Nah, can't be."*

"Does Jackie talk about us much?" Leaky asked.

"He said that you were all major villains like him."

"Oh did he?" Brian said.

"But I had heard about you, Al, long before I met Jackie."

"I think she just gave me that certain look," Al thought. *"Is she letting me know that she's available?"*

"There you go," Jackie said as he put the tray on the table.

"Cheers," Leaky said as he reached over for the lager.

"Yeah cheers," Al said, raising his glass.

Brian just nodded his head.

As the evening progressed, Al and the Combination were joined by a further twelve business associates. Jackie appeared to be relishing being amongst Kings Cross hierarchy. Margaret had everyone's attention as she crossed and uncrossed her long, shapely, legs.

"Hello, what's all this then?" Leaky said, as a broad six-foot six-inch giant of a man with the powerful physique of a rugby player, walked into the pub. He wore a tight white polo shirt and blue bleached jeans with brown slip on shoes.

The man looked around the pub and finally rested his eyes on where Al and his group of friends were sitting.

"He must be brave or some kind of bloody idiot to be strutting about on his own like that in here," Al thought as the man approached their table.

"You, O'Docherty!" the man called out.

Al and the Combination sat upright.

"I'm not scared of anyone, least of all you, so we will not be paying a single penny for protection."

Jackie turned casually to face him.

"I'm not looking for trouble," the man said as he looked at those around Al individually. "But I ain't paying fuck all to anyone, especially not to some runt of the litter."

Jackie was up and out of his seat. He threw a powerful left jab followed by two rapid right hooks. Then he stepped back, took aim, and launched a kick right between the legs. The man gasped and fell forward. Jackie grabbed him by the ears and pulled his face into his own.

"Arghhhh!" the man cried out as Jackie bit down on his lip before tearing it clean of his face.

The man fell to his knees while cupping his face and crying out with the intense pain. Jackie kicked him over and began to stamp on his face and head.

"Get this piece of shit out of here," Jackie said after spitting the man's lip out on the floor.

Two of the regulars grabbed him by the arms, dragged him out onto the street, and left him outside leaning against the wall. When they returned one of the men said "Now don't go taking any of his lip."

Brian began to laugh.

"He won't be giving anyone any lip again," said another.

Sid picked up the lip and placed it against his own.

"Hmm I love you," he joked while pretending to kiss it.

"Over here," Brian called out.

The lip was thrown over and Brian managed to catch it with his foot. He kicked it up into the air with his right foot and then caught it skilfully with his left.

"Over to you," Brian called out before kicking the lip over to Leaky who only managed to keep it up for two kicks before allowing it to fall onto the floor.

"Fuck it!" Al shouted before stamping his foot down on the lip.

The doors to the pub swung open and two paramedics raced in. One carried a box of ice.

"Where is his lip?" the paramedic called out.

"Please, help me, help me," said the second.

"There it is," Al said gingerly.

The paramedic looked down at the shrivelled piece of torn flesh. He looked up at Al and then to all those standing around him.

"You people are fucking animals!"

The pub fell silent.

"What kind of people could do something like that?"

Chapter 6

Al had just sunk his third pint and needed to take a pee. He sauntered through the bar to the men's toilets at the Bell pub. Inside he spotted a man leaning over the toilet cubicle sniffing a line of cocaine. The figure stood upright, sniffed loudly and proceeded to rub his finger around his mouth.

"Alright Al."

The cocaine sniffer was Jimmy Connelly. Jimmy liked to hang around pubs with major villains. He liked to buy his way in with rounds on him and splashing cash around. His scaffolding business provided a good living, and his criminal activities placed him high up on the earners that Al knew about. On a weekly basis, Jimmy would go to a local labour exchange, give a false name, and tell them that he needed between ten and fifteen men for a day's work for between fifteen and twenty pounds. A transit van would take the unemployed men out to a building site. They would be given hand tools to take down the scaffolding and stack it on an open back truck. Meanwhile, Jimmy would sit in a café or bar with a view nearby, and watch them dismantle the scaffolding. The unemployed men, desperate for work and an income, had no idea that they were stealing the scaffolding, and in the unlikely event they were challenged, Jimmy would just drive away. The transit van and the open back truck were both stolen and ran on false number plates for each job.

It was a sweet racket that had been earning Jimmy over five thousand pounds most weeks. Al admired what Jimmy was doing because it was smart and delivered serious cash. He had, on occasions, considered taxing Jimmy to the tune of one thousand pounds a week.

Al nodded and began to pee.

"I've got plenty if you fancy a line."

"Nah, I'm alright thanks Jimmy." Al said as he shook his member and placed it back inside his trousers.

Jimmy's best friend from school had overdosed on cocaine but still Jimmy snorted it daily.

Al took one last look in the cubicle as Jimmy bent over the cistern and began snorting another line. He shook his head and traipsed off back into the busy bar.

Al, from the corner of his eye, spotted a young girl checking him out.

She was about nineteen with a thin, svelte figure that chalice shaped her waist. Her tresses of moon-shadow black hair surged and flowed over her dainty shoulders.

Al returned to his seat and picked up his pint glass.

"You're Al McIntosh aren't you?"

Al looked up to see the girl who had been checking him out. Her effervescent champagne brown eyes were dew pond round and her young bee-stung lips were sugar plum sweet and satin soft.

"I am."

"I've heard about you."

"All good I hope."

"Mostly, but not all of it."

Al took a sip from his lager.

"My name is Christine, can I sit down?"

"You're forward," Al thought as he watched her short blue chequered skirt rise up as she sat down.

Al smiled.

"Is it true what people say about you?"

Al shrugged his shoulders and sat back in his chair as *'Going Underground'* by The Jam played in the background.

"That would depend on what "they" are supposed to have said."

"My friends have said that you're a dangerous man and nothing moves in Kings Cross that you don't know about or have a stake in."

Al chuckled.

"I'm a businessman who sometimes provides security to ensure that my client's customers are safe and keep spending."

"You're in protection, I knew it," Christine said.

Al took a sip of his lager.

"That's not a word I would use."

"Who is this girl?" Al thought as her skirt hitched up further.

"My friend, Janice, said that you and her… well you know."

"Really, Janice?" Al thought. *"I know a couple of Janice's, but none her age."*

"She said that you did something that no one had ever done to her before."

"What was that then?" Al said with a smile.

Christine leaned forward and lowered her voice to whisper.

"That's very possible," Al said with a chuckle.

"Christine!"

Al turned to see Jimmy Connelly, red faced and stomping towards the table.

"Shit, it's my dad," Christine said, rolling her eyes.

Al sat back in his chair.

"I don't want you having anything to do with him," Jimmy said, stabbing his finger at Christine.

"Who do you think you are, telling me who I should and shouldn't see?"

"I'm your father and you live in my house, so you will do exactly what I say!"

"I'm nineteen, Dad, and all grown up," Christine said, rising abruptly to her feet. "If I want to see Al then I will, and there is nothing you can do about it."

"Fuck me, I'm just having a quiet pint and all this kicks off," Al thought as he watched the father and daughter argue.

"He's a villain and you're not seeing him now or ever," Jimmy yelled out. "I don't give a flying fuck how old you are, you'll do what I say!"

"A villain! That's rich coming from you!"

"I don't want you seeing my daughter, Al!"

"I'm not, we were just chatting."

"I know you and I know what you're like, and you're not going to carve another notch on your bedpost with my daughter."

"Calm down, we were just chatting."

"No, Al, this is a matter of principle," Christine said, putting her hands on her hips. "Being your daughter doesn't give you the right to tell me what I can and can't do, period!"

"I thought we were mates, Al!"

"You like hanging around me because of who I am," Al thought.

"Go home, now!" Jimmy ordered as *'Poison Ivy'* by The Lambrettas played on the jukebox.

"No!" Christine shouted, before stomping her right foot on the floor.

"If you don't leave here right now, young lady, I promise you there will be big trouble."

Christine looked down at Al for support but there was none.

Al took a sip of his lager, peered past Jimmy and motioned the barman to bring him over another drink.

Christine huffed heavily, stamped her foot on the floor again, swivelled rapidly on her heels and marched through the pub out onto the street.

"I thought you would know better," Jimmy said, looking down at Al.

"She came on to me."

Jimmy spun around and strode back to the toilets.

"Twat," Al thought as he watched him disappear behind the door.

Al later learned that the Metropolitan police had set up a special task force to track down the scaffolding thefts and categorised it as 'organised crime'.

Chapter 7

"There you go," Leaky said as he handed Nicky a bundle of fresh counterfeit five-pound notes.

"Thanks Leaky," Nicky replied before kissing Leaky on the cheek.

"You're keeping busy then?"

"There's no end of punters," Nicky replied with a girlie giggle. "This is Kings Cross."

"No place in the world like it," Leaky said as he placed the remaining wad of notes into his trouser pocket.

"Did you hear about Fat Julie?"

"Fat Julie?"

"Yeah you know, Fat Julie, she works all the kinky stuff."

Yeah, yeah, I think so. She's not a regular customer to me."

"I'm not surprised, because she works with the upmarket lot, you know politicians, bankers and that."

"So what happened?"

Nicky ran her fingers through the swirls of her caramel-brown hair before taking a deep breath.

"Well, Julie had been seeing this old banker geezer. He must have been in his late sixties according to her. He would turn up at her place once a month and duly hand over one hundred pounds."

"A hundred quid for a shag?"

Nicky giggled.

"There's more."

"I should bloody well hope so for a hundred quid."

"Well this banker geezer likes something a bit, should we say, different."

"Really?" Leaky said with a wry grin.

"Oh yeah," Nicky said with a chuckle. "Julie has this special glass top coffee table and this old banker likes to strip off naked and then lie under the table."

"Go on," Leaky persisted.

"Well, Fat Julie crouches over the table, grits her teeth, and proceeds to take a shit."

"Urgh, you're having me on."

"No, straight up. Once a month he pays Fat Julie to shit over the glass top coffee table while he wanks himself off.

"That's fucking horrible."

"We get some strange requests out here," Nicky said, shaking her head. "Anyway the old banker is urging her on her while he's bashing one out and Fat Julie has lost her balance."

"No."

"Yeah, Fat Julie and her seventeen stone have fallen smack down onto the glass and it shattered, big time."

"No way," Leaky said with a wince.

"The glass has shattered into small pieces and it tore, sliced and got stuck in both Fat Julie's arse and the old banker's face, and he is covered in blood."

Leaky started to laugh as he visualised the carnage.

"What happened?"

"Well they've both had to go to the hospital," Nicky said. "Can you imagine that old banker going home to explain that one?"

"It doesn't bear thinking about."

REV... REV... SCREECH...

Leaky and Nicky turned sharply to see a bright red Ford Capri breaking out sideways with tyre smoke belching out of its arches. People in the road stepped back as the Ford Capri came to a screeching halt outside the Scottish Stores pub.

"Fucking idiot," Leaky muttered.

"Anyway, thanks for the fivers, Leaky," Nicky said before turning sharply. "I'll see you again next week."

"Yeah sure," Leaky said as he watched John, Al's brother, climb out of the Ford Capri.

"I might have fucking known," Leaky muttered to himself.

John slammed the Capri Door shut before straightening up and inhaling deeply.

"John," Leaky called out.

"Hello mate, what do you think of the new wheels?"

Leaky cast his eyes over the bright red three litre V6 Ford Capri.

"It's loud and obnoxious," Leaky said. "It cries out attention seeker."

"Well I think it's brilliant."

"We need to have a quiet word," Leaky said in a quiet, serious, tone.

John rolled his eyes.

"Don't you go fucking rolling your eyes at me," Leaky said firmly. "I've been hearing about you strutting about like some kind of peacock giving people right handers."

"I didn't slap anyone that didn't have it coming."

Leaky stepped back and looked John up and down.

"Who the fuck do you think you are?"

John remained silent.

"You're a fucking painter and decorator, John, and you are certainly not your brother!"

"I never said I was!"

"People are giving you respect around here because of Al. This is an extremely dangerous place, John, and if you keep that kind of shit up then somebody will put you in the ground."

Leaky took a step closer with his eyes firmly fixed on John.

"I didn't mean anything by it," John replied.

"I didn't think so."

John turned and opened the door to his Ford Capri. He clambered inside and turned the ignition on. The big, throaty, V6 engine let out a ferocious roar. John slammed the door shut, wound down the window and turned the Sharp stereo on. *'Start'* by The Jam pounded out from the speakers.

Leaky shook his head slowly as John rammed the gear shifter into first gear, revved the powerful engine and dropped the clutch. The tyres screeched as burning grey smoke belched out from both rear wheel arches. The Capri slid away sideways leaving two thick black tyre marks on the road outside the pub.

"This is the kind of attention we don't need," Leaky muttered to himself.

Leaky stepped inside the pub, acknowledged the working girls at the bar before sauntering over to join Al and Brian at their usual table.

"Alright Leaky," Al said as Leaky pulled out his chair.

Once Al had motioned the barman to bring over a round of drinks, Leaky proceeded to tell Al how his brother had been capitalising on his reputation around Kings Cross and giving out right handers.

"I'll have a word," Al said as the barman placed the tray of drinks on the table.

"We've got a bit of problem," the barman said.

"What's the problem?" Al replied before taking a sip of his lager.

"Somebody in here has nicked the main raffle prize."

The landlord held regular raffles and used the takings to help out the families of his regulars when their husbands get sent down.

"What was it?"

"A turkey," the barman replied.

Leaky and Brian chuckled.

"Who would want to nick a turkey?" Al said with a snigger. "Here," Al said as he handed the barman a twenty pound note. "Go and get the biggest turkey you can find."

"That's not the point," the barman persisted.

Al placed his drink on the table and looked up into the barman's eyes.

"The clientele here are murderers, armed robbers, thieves, fraudsters, hookers, villains and violent gangsters. No one is going to grass on the person who nicked the bloody turkey. Whoever took it was either in need of it or did it for a laugh. Either way it's gone and I suggest you take that money, replace the stolen turkey, and say no more about it."

"Yes, Al," the barman replied sheepishly.

"What's his name?" Al asked.

"Duncan," Leaky replied.

"I was in here the other night and there were two lads at the bar who were clearly just here for a drink and to find a girl. Anyway, these lads had a couple and were buying these girls drinks, when Duncan has refused to serve one of the lads stating that he had enough because he couldn't even look at him straight."

"What?"

"That's not the best of it. This lad's mate has had to point out that he's been cross-eyed since birth."

Leaky started to laugh with Al quickly following.

"It's not really that funny," Brian said with a dead pan expression which only made Leaky and Al laugh more.

Al motioned Duncan, the barman, to bring over another round of drinks.

"I've been hearing stuff about Jackie O'Docherty from a reliable source."

"Who?" Al said.

"A couple of the girls who buy my fivers told me. They thought we should know what was being said."

"I don't fucking like him," Brian said.

"No one does."

"Except that bird he has on the firm, what's her name…Margaret."

"She's bought and paid for."

"If I was a bird I wouldn't fuck that ugly bastard for anything."

"You would."

"Well maybe, but it would cost a lot."

"If you were a working girl, you'd drop your drawers for a pint of lager and a packet of cheese and onion crisps."

The three men laughed.

"Jackie has been having talks with Big Jim Gibson and Dougie 'The Man' McInnon."

Al's smile disappeared.

"What's been happening?"

"By all accounts Jackie is getting all pissed up and trying to get support from Big Jim and 'The Man' to take us out and take Kings Cross back."

"Carry on."

"From what the girls were saying, neither Big Jim Gibson nor Dougie 'The Man' McInnon had any interest in supporting him. He kept on going on about not being able to work the Cross and how it wasn't fair. Nonetheless, we'll need to keep an eye on Jackie O'Docherty."

"Give me the word and I'll put him in the ground," Brian growled through gritted teeth.

"He's just licking his wounds," Al said. "If he was serious he would have been in here by now with a shooter. We'll keep an eye on him, like you say, Leaky, but we don't have to get too serious just yet."

The pub door opened and John stepped in with a tall blonde on his arm. He kissed her on the cheek and watched as she joined the other working girls by the bar.

"I'm starving," Leaky said, rubbing his stomach.

"Half a dozen beers will do that," Al said with a chuckle.

"I suppose a Chinese is out of the question?"

"I would suggest we give it a swerve for the time being."

"Why, what happened at the Chinese?" John asked excitedly.

"That's a story for another time," Al said before knocking back his whiskey chaser.

"I've been hearing good things about that Turkish place, The Anatolian."

"What's that then?"

"They do all sorts of delicious grilled meats and salads with apricot, mint and pomegranate."

"Yeah, why not," Al said as he rose from his chair.

Al, Leaky, Brian and John left the Scottish Stores and made their way over to the Anatolian Restaurant on the Grays Inn Road.

John got out his car keys.

"We're not going in that," Al said as he looked at the bright red Ford Capri. "Besides, you've been drinking."

John put the keys back in his pocket and followed the men.

The Anatolian was a popular restaurant with the Turkish Cypriot community in Islington. Al had passed it many times but never ventured in.

Leaky opened and held the door open.

Al was instantly smitten by the stunning, breath taking woman walking towards them.

"Wow, she is simply divine," Al thought as his eyes met hers.

"Welcome to The Anatolian," the woman purred.

"She's stylish, elegant and captivating!" Al thought as he shook the woman's hand.

"I'm Al McIntosh. This is Leaky, and these are my brothers Brian and John."

"It's very nice to meet you Al. I am Toprak Ercel, that is my husband, Emin, at the bar, and this is our restaurant.

"Shit, she's married," Al thought as he found himself staring into her alluring, vivacious brown eyes.

"Please follow me," Toprak said as she turned swiftly on her black leather high heels and led the friends towards a table by the window.

Al watched as her slim, sculpted, hour-glass shaped figure wriggled suggestively from left to right within her elegant knee length dress.

Al was captivated.

"Toprak, what a charming name," Al thought as he sat on the chair closest to the window. *"What an exquisite beauty."*

"Would you gentlemen like a drink while you look at the menu?"

"Toprak's olive bronze complexion is flawless and her melodious voice is syrup sweet," Al thought as he stared up at her lavish locks of coral black hair that toppled over her shoulders and nestled on her voluptuous cleavage.

"What drinks would you suggest?" Al said.

Toprak's succulent, sultry and velvet soft lips parted, revealing unicorn white teeth and a cherubic smile.

Al could feel his heart racing.

"Damn, why does she have to be married?" Al thought.

"The national drink of Turkey is Raki," Toprak said, handing them each a food menu. "It is made from twice distilled grapes from the western Anatolian regions and generally drunk with still water."

"I would crawl to the western Anatolian regions on my hands and knees just to spend an evening in your company," Al thought, returning her smile.

"Raki sounds perfect, we'll have a bottle, thank you."

Toprak held Al's intense gaze for a few seconds before returning to the bar.

"I think she fancies me," Al thought as he opened his menu. *"Or is she just being friendly? There was something in that smile, something special, I'm sure of it."*

"I wanted a lager," John said.

"We're in a Turkish restaurant, so be adventurous," Al said with a stern look.

John sulked.

Moments later Toprak returned with a tray. She placed a bottle of Raki and a jug of cold water on the table. A waiter had followed her across the restaurant. He placed a selection of delicious mezzes, white cheese, butter and a fresh balloon bread on the table.

"People often think that Raki is served with the main dish, but in Turkey it is enjoyed most when served with a fine selection of mezzes and good company."

"Thank you," Al said, putting the food menu on the table. "I've never experienced Turkish food before. What would you recommend?"

"I'd like to eat this mezze from your naked body," Al thought, running his eyes up and down Toprak's shapely figure.

"I would suggest a mixed grill. It'll include tender cubes of chicken, lamb and beef that have been marinated in our special house sauce and grilled on skewers. The main course will include rice, salad, red peppers, onion, garlic, parsley and yoghurt cucumber sauce."

"Will there be any chips?" John asked.

Toprak smiled and shook her head.

"We don't do chips I'm afraid, but we can include our Mediterranean mashed potato."

"Sounds perfect," Al said as he looked over at Leaky and then at Brian.

"Yeah, sounds great." Leaky replied with a chuckle. "I could eat a horse."

"We serve good sized portions," Toprak said with a warm chuckle.

Al found himself following her perfectly manicured Aphrodite red fingernails as she took the menus.

Suddenly a shock tore through Al's body as her slender fingers brushed lightly against his skin.

"She's making a connection," Al thought as he looked up into her alluring brown eyes. *"That was a signal, I'm sure of it."*

"Can I have a pint of lager, please?" John asked.

"Of course," Toprak said.

Leaky poured the Raki and then filled the glass with the cold water.

"I've had this before," Leaky said as he raised his glass. "The Turks in Islington call this the Lion's Milk."

Al took a sip.

"I like it," Al said before taking a slightly longer sip. "It tastes a bit like Pernod."

"I wouldn't make that comparison to a Turk," Leaky said with a chuckle. "It's their national drink."

A waiter returned to the table carrying a pint glass and a large bottle of Efes lager.

"Cheers," John said as he reached for the glass.

"Have you worked here long?" Al asked the waiter.

"About ten months."

"Are you enjoying it?"

"Very much."

"Good," Al said with a smile. "What is Emin like to work for?"

"He is very fair."

"And Toprak?"

"Mrs Ercel is more than fair, sir," the waiter said before leaving.

The four men tucked into their mezzes and sipped the Raki.

"Do you fancy her?" Leaky whispered.

"She's married," Al whispered back.

"So are most of the brasses around Kings Cross."

"That's different."

"She fancies you."

"You reckon?"

"Absolutely."

Al smiled and drank the last of his Raki.

The mezze dishes were taken away and replaced with trays of sizzling grilled meats.

"I need this," Leaky said as he reached over for a lamb chop.

Al took a bite from the chicken shish and then placed his knife and fork by the side of the plate.

"I'm just going to have a pee," Al said as he rose from the table.

Al strode across the restaurant. He looked over at Toprak's husband, Emin, who was busy chatting with two customers at the bar.

"Is everything okay?"

Al turned back to see Toprak standing in front of him.

"Yes, I just need the gents."

Toprak smiled.

"I'll show you."

Al glanced back at Emin who was now drinking with his customers and then turned back to follow Toprak through the restaurant and out into a hallway.

Al stood by the toilet door.

"I think you might like me," Toprak said with an alluring smile.

"I think you're stunning," Al replied as his heart thumped against his chest. "It's such a shame that you're married."

"I don't fancy taking on the Turkish mafia over an adventurous liaison," Al thought as he held her gaze. *"All these guys are connected by family one way or another."*

Toprak giggled.

"Emin and I have an arrangement."

"What does she mean, arrangement?" Al thought as the blood raced around his body and into his loins.

Toprak reached out and took Al's hand in hers.

"My husband occasionally meets with other woman."

"I'm sorry," Al said.

"That is our agreement," Toprak said with a suggestive smile. "Emin is free to pursue sex or an emotional relationship with other people, and I am free to do the same. We have an open relationship and it works well for us both."

"And you are okay with this?"

Toprak nodded.

"I find it hard to believe that your husband would agree to you seeking a relationship with someone else. Does he not get jealous?"

Toprak chuckled and squeezed Al's hand.

"Our mutual arrangement provides benefits for us both. Both Emin and I enjoy the novelty when it comes to sexuality. If we are all honest, we all crave something new and different at times and I am no different to Emin with those feelings.

"Fuck me, I've hit the jackpot here," Al thought as his manhood pressed firmly against his trousers.

"For it to work successfully both Emin and I have to be very open and honest with each other and we share a deepened sense of trust. I love my husband, Al McIntosh, and would never consider leaving him, but I do need to express my needs and identity without fear from time to time. Hiding a crush or an affair can be distressing, but by being open it can only strengthen your relationship."

"I think that sounds incredibly liberated of you both."

"It also sounds too bloody good to be true, what's the catch?" Al thought.

"Are you honestly saying that your husband has never been jealous?"

"No, and neither have I."

"This is like something out of a dirty magazine," Al thought.

"So, Al McIntosh, do you like me?"

"I would walk over burning coals for you," Al said with a nervous chuckle.

"That won't be necessary," Toprak said as she let go of Al's hand, smiled and then left the hallway.

Al stood in front of the cubicle.

"She a stunning girl, how can her old man allow her to go out and just have sex with other men and not get jealous?" Al thought as he strained to pee. *"Then again, isn't that the kind of relationship that Black Sandra and I have, and it works for us?"*

Finally Al was able to pee.

"About bloody time."

Al washed his hands and returned to his friends. He glanced over at Emin who was clinking glasses with his customers.

"Is he going to be hiding in the wardrobe watching us while we're at it?" Al thought. *"Then again, I wouldn't give two hoots if it meant a few hours with the gorgeous and available Toprak."*

"You're definitely on there," Leaky whispered.

"I know," Al replied with a chuckle.

"Nice one!"

The four men ate their meals and enjoyed Baklava, a layered filo pastry dessert made with chopped nuts and sweetened syrup with a traditional Turkish coffee.

Toprak brought the bill to the table.

"I'll take care of this," Al said, peeling off several notes from his wad.

"Cheers."

"Thanks."

"Thank you Toprak for a truly delicious meal. We shall certainly be back," Leaky said.

Toprak handed Al a note and smiled. He stood up and whispered into her ear.

"Are you sure your husband is okay with this? I don't want to end up on the sharp end of a kebab knife?"

"Would you like me to bring him over?"

"No, no, that's not necessary."

Toprak walked with the men to the door and held it open.

"I hope, very much, to see you again," Toprak said with her vivacious brown eyes fixed firmly on Al. "Soon."

"Fancy a couple at the Stores?" Brian said as he put his hands in his trouser pockets.

"Yeah, why not," Leaky said before belching loudly. "Pardon me."

"Nah, I'm on a promise," John said while puffing out his chest.

"Good for you," Al said.

"Yeah, remember that blonde I was with earlier?"

"Yes, that's Tammy, and I've been there," Al thought. *"Lovely little thing and does a great turn for twenty quid."*

Al nodded.

"Well she has this friend, Monica, and they're both up for a threesome," John said raising his eyebrows.

"I've caught that show," Brian said. "Have fun."

"Me too," Leaky said as they crossed the busy London Street.

Al watched as John's chest slowly became deflated.

"Take no notice of those pair of windups," Al said while winking at Brian. "You only live once so enjoy yourself."

"Yeah, I will," John said before racing ahead. "See you later."

Al looked back at the Anatolian Restaurant while feeling the unread note in his pocket. He stopped.

"I'll catch you both up," Al said.

"Alright, see you later," Brian said.

Leaky smiled then caught up with Brian.

Al took the note from his pocket and read:

Al McIntosh call me x

A telephone number was written underneath.

"When should I call her? It doesn't say." Al thought as he stared down at the note.

From the corner of his eye he spotted a red telephone box.

"I'll do it now," Al thought as the image of the beautiful Toprak forced its way to the front of his mind.

Al raced over to the telephone box, opened the door and lifted the receiver. He dialled the number and waited until the pips sounded before putting the coin in the phone.

UNKNOWN: Good evening, this is the Anatolian Restaurant, how can I help you?"

AL: Good evening can I speak to Toprak please.

UNKNOWN: Toprak?

AL: Yes, Mrs Ercel.

UNKNOWN: Certainly sir.

Al closed his eyes and rubbed his forehead.

"This is like something out of a movie," Al thought while he waited.

TOPRAK: Hello, this is Mrs Toprak Ercel, how can I help you?

AL: Hello Toprak, its Al.

Al could hear Toprak chuckle.

TOPRAK: Well you certainly took your time.

AL: Are you okay to talk?

TOPRAK: I am.

AL: How would you like to go out sometime to grab a meal or something?

TOPRAK: I would prefer the... or something. What are you doing tonight?

"Wow that was forward," Al thought as his mouth went dry.

AL: I don't have anything planned.

TOPRAK: Do you know the Crestfield Hotel in Crestfield Street?

AL: I do.

TOPRAK: Why don't you book us a room and we'll have a bit of room service.

AL could feel his heart battering against his chest.

AL: I can do that.

TOPRAK: Book the room in your name and I'll be with you around 11.00 okay?

AL: I'll go and book it now.

TOPRAK: Good, because I'm looking forward to seeing you later.

The phone went dead.

"Damn, I only came out for something to eat," Al thought as he placed the receiver back.

Al checked his watch and then raced around to the Crestfield Hotel and booked a double room. He asked for a bottle of champagne to be sent to the room with two champagne flutes. Al opened the window and breathed in the cold London air.

During his time in Soho and Kings Cross, Al had come to understand that amongst the everyday people, erotic thoughts and fantasies were often followed by feelings of shame, guilt and self-loathing. Most people grow up harangued by the local vicar or other religious leaders and self-styled guardians of morality who preach that among the many sexual possibilities only a few are morally acceptable within a monogamous, married, relationship. A great many of the men that had sex with the working girls of Kings Cross had never received or given oral sex, explored new positions, or had been limited to sex once a month.

Kings Cross offered sex with different races and ethnicities. Older men preferred young girls while young men sought the experience of the older women who knew how to please. Al had many conversations with the working girls and they told him that most of the men they saw fantasised about having sex with multiple partners, which was why some of the girls worked together to act out threesomes for a premium. Al was a little shocked when he discovered that some of the girls had secretly had the same fantasy before leaving their home towns to become working girls. Senior management, bankers and politicians were the bread and butter for the girls who offered bondage, discipline and sado-masochism, while other men were turned on by the fear of being caught having sex in cars, parks and pub toilets.

Al was of the opinion that all sexual fantasies were normal, healthy and sex-enhancing.

"*Toprak is refreshing, flamboyant and very clear about what she wants,*" Al thought before laughing the thought away as he gazed out the window.

He looked down at the bucket of ice that held the champagne bottle.

"*Damn, it's melting,*" Al thought.

There was a knock at the door.

"*Could that be Emin and she lied about the whole open relationship thing and just gets off on jealousy?*" Al thought as he clenched his fist. "*No, don't be silly.*"

Al took a couple of steps towards the door and opened it.

Toprak stood in the Hallway.

"Wow, you look fabulous," Al said as he motioned for her to enter the room.

"Thank you," Toprak replied with a suggestive smile.

Toprak closed the door and turned towards Al.

Chapter 8

Al had not been sitting for long at his usual table at the King Charles the First Pub in Northdown Street when Dundee Ged approached his table.

The pub had been nicknamed the Jerry Bar, because during the war men would take their jerry cans there and fill them with beer.

Dundee Ged had been found not guilty of a contract killing and so those around Kings Cross assumed and spread rumours that he was a contract killer and had carried out scores of murders all over the country. Al didn't know if it was true and privately thought that Dundee Ged was a bit of an idiot, but those around the Cross certainly believed it to be.

A contract killing is a form of murder or assassination where one party hires another party to kill a person.

Al looked up as Dundee Ged placed two thousand pounds in cash on the table. Al smiled and quickly gathered the cash up and slipped it into his pocket. Ged pulled up a chair and sat opposite Al.

"Nice one," Al thought, tapping his pocket.

"Jimmy Connelly paid me four thousand quid to take you out," Dundee Ged said.

"Drink?" Al said calmly.

"Whiskey."

Al motioned the barman to bring over a fresh tray of drinks.

"I don't know what you did to fuck him off, but he wants you dead."

"It's a long story," Al said casually.

"I took the contract but have decided not to see it through."

The barman placed the tray of drinks on the table before rushing back to serve his other customers.

"I figured that it would only be a question of time before you found out," Dundee Ged said. "Villains are renowned for being big mouths and I don't need the aggravation."

Al looked up at Dundee Ged's cold brown eyes with a manic smile.

"So it's two grand for you and two grand for me, which leaves me and you square."

Al reached out and shook his hand.

"Jimmy Connelly can swivel for his money."

"Fuck him," Al said casually.

"Yeah, fuck him."

Dundee Ged rose from the table and then swallowed his whiskey in one gulp.

"See you about."

Al nodded and raised his whiskey tumbler.

Leaky bounded over from the bar carrying a drink in each hand.

"Not like you to employ his services," Leaky said with a chuckle.

"Nah, it's nothing like that."

Out of the corner of his eye, Al saw his sister, Doreen, enter the pub arm in arm with Graham Pearson, also known as 'Leeds', a local social worker who also dealt in heroin. Leeds had a solid reputation as a guy who helped the working girls fight their cases and was a go too guy for cheap heroin. Non-payers were subjected to savage violence.

Doreen had been living with a barman known as PJ in Glasgow. He had been christened with the nick name after telling the pub's customers how taken he was with Disney's Robin Hood movie, and went to the cinema to see it four times. One of the key characters in the movie was Prince John, a Lion, who was also called PJ. The name had stuck. PJ had promised Doreen the world. He shared his big plans to move up in the world and Doreen decided that she wanted to share that journey. She fell pregnant and shortly after the baby was born, she packed her bags and took the Glasgow train down to London. PJ had failed to deliver on the life she had been expecting and there would be no second chances. PJ arrived home from work to find Doreen and his daughter gone. Al was staggered by her mercenary outlook on relationships, but helped her to get onto her feet with a home and some money in her pocket, and it wasn't long before she took up with Tommy Buchannon.

Tommy Buchannon had arrived in London from his home town of Dublin a few years earlier. He used his criminal connections to secure a reliable, low cost, source of heroin and then shipped the product back to Dublin. Tommy was making big money and was smitten with the beautiful Doreen. For a while they ate and drank, spending the money as fast as it was coming in. However, when Tommy started to use his own heroin, he became careless and unreliable. Business took a dramatic downturn. Tommy became an addict and as quickly as he won Doreen, he lost her. Tommy ended up in a squat with two other addicts. They shared heroin and needles. One of the addicts took a batch of pills back to the squat and Tommy began to overdose. The junkies carried Tommy down the flight of chairs and sat him in a chair in the hallway before packing up the few possessions they had and left Kings Cross. Al was outraged by the callousness of their actions, and had gone looking for them. He liked Tommy and had been buying him drinks when he was skint. When Tommy's dealer turned up, Al tried to talk Tommy into moving in with him but he left with the dealer.

Tommy had been left alone to die.

"How did you get on with that that Turkish bird?" Leaky said as he placed the tray of lagers and whiskey chasers on the table.

Al looked and smiled.

"She was the fuck of the century."

"Coming from you she must have been a bit special," Leaky said as he sat down. "Is she on the firm now or what?"

Al shook his head and took a sip of his drink.

"No, it'll be a one, maybe a two time thing, and she's made that quite clear," Al lied.

"I'll keep that going for as long as possible," Al thought.

"Lovely looking girl," Leaky said.

"She certainly is that."

"Are you here for the night?"

"I'll have this and then pop along to a birthday party."

"Birthday party?"

"Yeah, you know Tammy, the blonde? It's her birthday so she's having a few people over for drinks. You should come."

"Nah, I've got a bit of work lined up with the South London lads, Bootsie and Smudge."

Bootsie and Smudge had been buying large quantities of cheque books from Leaky. The lads had a team of girls cashing them in all over London. The venture had been so successful that the lads became Leaky's only customers for both the cheque books and the Euro-Cheques. Their teams were taking a train down to Dover and doing a day trip on the ferry over to Calais and Dunkirk, France. One married couple from the Ledbury Estate in Peckham had rented a flat in Calais so the cheque books could be posted out to avoid any potential issues at customs.

"Give them my best," Al said before looking down at his watch.

"Did you hear about the dodgy cider?"

Al shook his head.

"Bootsie was telling me that a couple of lively lads from New Cross had turned over a warehouse and made off with half a truck load of cider. They could tell it had been sitting about for a while, so they put a hose over the pallet to make it more saleable."

"Cider you say."

"Yeah. Anyway the boys have flogged it to a spieler in Lewisham. The landlord is made up with his cheap booze and the lads have made a few quid. Anyway, the landlord has stuck this cider up on a special, so everyone in the pub is knocking it back. About an hour has passed and one of the men complained about a stomach ache before ripping off this long and loud toxic fart. A couple of the boys laughed, while others fanned their faces and told him to take it outside. Another hour and half in the spieler and punters are clutching their stomachs and cracking off. By all accounts the place was pungent and stunk like a pig farm on a hot day."

"Nasty," Al said as he sipped his lager.

"It gets worse."

"This one bird, the girlfriend of a known face, was standing at the bar and she is trying desperately to let this ripper out silently. Bootsie reckons that there was a four-foot safety zone around her and then... she's followed through."

"No way."

Leaky laughed out loud.

"Al, by all accounts it was awful. The poor cow has not only filled her drawers but it just kept on coming. Drinkers have run for cover and this poor girl is just standing by the bar in her Sunday best clobber and crying her eyes out with steaming hot shit running down her legs."

"We're not putting any knocked off cider in our spielers," Al said, scrunching up his face. "What happened to the lads who put the dodgy gear in there?"

"They were paid a visit, given a slap and had to return the money plus a bit of compensation to the face and his girlfriend."

Al emptied the last of his pint and placed it on the table.

"I might see you back in here later," Al said as he rose from the table.

"Enjoy the birthday cake," Leaky said with a chuckle.

Al strolled through his criminal empire with his chest firmly stuck out. He breathed in the Kings Cross air while nodding and acknowledging the faces and working girls that passed by. Tammy's flat was on the third floor of a four storey house. The front door was open, so he stepped inside. He could hear *'I'm in the Mood for Dancing'* by the Nolans, and followed the sound up to the third floor.

KNOCK KNOCK

The door opened almost immediately.

"Happy birthday Tammy," Al said as he handed her a roll of ten pound notes. "Thank you for the invite."

Tammy threw her arms around him.

"Thank you and I'm so pleased that you've come."

The song changed to *'Too Hot'* by Kool & The Gang.

Al followed Tammy through the hallway and into the lounge. There were several girls that he recognised all dancing together. John, his brother, was dancing with Monica, Tammy's new flatmate and Brian was chatting to one of Black Sandra's friends, Valerie.

"Hello Al, here you go mate, have a drink."

Sid, Tom and Ron, from the Chinese meat cleaver incident, were chatting together.

"Cheers," Al said before knocking back the neat whiskey in one go.

"We were just talking about the universe and death and how it's impossible to believe that we're the only living creatures," Sid said as he refilled Al's glass. "Ron reckons that there could be all sorts of creatures out there. What's your take on it?"

"I suppose it's lucky that the universe and distances between planets is so vast that we're unlikely ever to be visited."

Sid nodded his head.

"Tom reckons that visitors from other worlds are already here and living among us."

"Probably, and they most likely drink at the Stores," Al said with a chuckle.

Tom drank his whiskey and then refilled his glass.

"The thing is, if we are supposed to have evolved from apes, then why are there still apes?"

Al looked over his shoulder and saw that John was now dancing with Sandy and Brian was still chatting.

"What's your theory?"

"Well I reckon that the earth was visited by intelligent aliens hundreds of thousands of years ago and they did some kind of surgery on humans so that we became self-aware and that spawned the species as it is today."

"What if the aliens just shagged the apes?" Ron asked.

"It's possible," Tom replied.

"I wouldn't want to shag an ape," Sid said, pulling a face of utter disgust.

"I need to exit this conversation," Al thought.

"They could come back any time," Tom said, sipping his whiskey.

"Most movies show the aliens being the aggressive invaders and humans as the good guys. We're not."

"We're not what?"

"People; you, me and everyone on this planet are not the good guys. We have wars that kill millions of men, women and children for power and control. People rob, kill and maim each other for a piece of paper with a picture of the Queen or an American president on it. Torture, rape and molestation all exist in every country around the world. The church, Borstals and reform schools all turn a blind eye to the sexual abuse carried out on children. If anything, we are the aggressors. The aliens, if they exist, have far more to fear from us than we do from them," Al said, looking over at Brian.

"I never thought about it like that," Tom said.

"We really are shit and not worth saving when you think about it," Ron said.

"It's good seeing you," Al said as he raised his glass. "I need to see my brother about a bit of business."

"Yeah, okay be lucky."

"Luck is nothing more than preparation meeting opportunity," Al thought as he strolled over to Brian.

"Have you heard from Sandy?"

"Yeah, she's doing okay."

"Good," Al replied.

Monica had rolled a marijuana joint and passed it to John.

"John seems happy enough," Brian said.

"We still need to keep an eye on him because he's not me and he's not you," Al said as they both watched John tug hard on the joint.

A couple of the girls had run a line of cocaine on the glass coffee table. They were both on their hands and knees in short mini-skirts snorting the white party powder while *'The Winner Takes it All'* by Abba played on the stereo.

"Nice," Al thought as he caught an eyeful of red panties.

Al stayed for a little over two hours before leaving the house party and returning to the Scottish Stores.

The drink and drugs flowed and the music got louder. With *'Oops Upside Your Head'* by the Gap Band booming out of the speakers, there was a succession of loud knocks on the door.

BANG! BANG! BANG! BANG!

Tammy opened the door and her drug dealing Liverpudlian neighbour, Leo Black, pushed past her in the hallway. He stomped down the hallway and into the lounge where he pushed past Monica and turned the volume down on the stereo.

"I have my wife and child downstairs and we can't hear ourselves think because your music is so fucking loud. Can you please just keep it down!"

Leo Black stood in the middle of the room for several seconds before stomping off back down the hallway.

"Who the fuck was that?" John said, looking directly at Monica.

"Our downstairs neighbour, Leo Black."

"Who does that Scouse wanker think he is?" John said, looking around the room.

"He's alright, really," Tammy said with an awkward smile.

"I fucking hate Scousers," John said.

"Just leave it John," one of the party guests said.

"Yeah, he's not worth it."

"He's not a bad bloke once you get to know him."

"I'll give him turn the fucking music down," John hissed, taking *'One Step Beyond'* by Madness out of its sleeve and placing it on the record deck.

"All Scousers deserve a right good kicking!" John said as he turned the volume up to maximum.

'Hey you don't watch that

Watch this

This is the heavy, heavy monster sound

The nuttiest sound around

So if you've come in off the street

And you're beginning to feel the heat

Well listen buster

You better start to move your feet

To rockiness, rock steady beat

Of Madness.

One Step Beyond'

The sounds of Madness filled the room. A couple of the men began to do the ska dance known as the skank, while others looked on, bobbing their heads back and forth.

While the music played, Leo Black raced across the lounge to the stereo and turned it down.

"I asked you nicely to please keep the music down!"

John watched intently as the Scouse drug dealer clenched and unclenched his fists.

Leo turned swiftly on his heels and left the party as quickly as he had arrived.

"Let's just keep it down a bit," Monica said.

"Yeah, we can still have a good time," Tammy said.

"It was hurting my ears," Sid said.

"I couldn't hear myself think," Tom said.

"No, fuck that Scouse bastard. If we want to play the music loud then we fucking well will, and he'll just have to live with it," John said as he placed *'I Only Want to Be With You'* by the Tourists on and wound the volume back to maximum again.

Moments later Leo Black pounded down the hallway and into the lounge. He had a bottle of cider in one hand and an eight-inch blade in the other.

"I fucking told you bastards to keep this shit down!" Leo shouted as he kicked the stereo system.

"That's enough," Brian said, stepping forward.

"Fuck you!" Leo yelled, slashing the knife wildly.

The razor sharp blade caught Brian and sliced his arm open. .

John raced forward and threw a mighty right hander. Brian looked down at the wound and let loose a rapid succession of left and right hooks. Leo dropped the bottle of cider as he staggered back from the barrage of powerful punches. Brian continued to pound Leo until he tripped and fell to the floor. John looked around and saw a hand held carpet cleaner. He raced over and picked it.

"You fucking Scouse bastard!" John yelled and brought the carpet cleaner down on Leo's head.

"You have no idea who you're dealing with!" John continued as he smashed the cleaner over Leo's head again and again.

"I'll show you who is who around here!" John cried out as he smashed the cleaner again and again with all his might.

The girls in the apartment screamed as the blood gushed from the horrific wounds.

A few of the men bolted for the door as John continued to relentlessly batter Leo's motionless body.

When John had finally stopped bashing the cleaner over the little of what was left of Leo's head, the blood had squirted and gushed over the carpet, furniture and walls. Tammy and Monica's front room looked like the inside of a busy abattoir.

John straightened himself and looked down at Leo's corpse.

"That fucking told him," John hissed before throwing the blood covered cleaner at the settee.

The girls were hysterical and most of the men had made a sharp exit. Brian looked up when he heard the police sirens. Within minutes the uniformed police officers crashed through the flat and battered both John and Brian to the floor with their truncheons.

Both John and Brian were arrested.

***

The remaining girls at the party all gave police statements. Leo Black's wife also gave a statement that said her husband had a short temper and was responsible for escalating a mild neighbourly dispute. The police, once they understood the crime had been committed by two of the McIntosh brothers, tried to talk Mrs Black into changing her statement.

The original charges of murder were dropped and replaced with manslaughter:

Brian McIntosh was sentenced to five years.

John McIntosh was sentenced to six years.

When Al visited his brothers at HMP Brixton, he told John that Leo did not have to die and certainly not in that barbaric manner. Al told John, in no uncertain terms, that he was out of order and had been a walking disaster since arriving in Kings Cross. He went on to say that Brian could have got the situation under control without the need to brutally murder Leo Black.

Chapter 9

"Doreen!"

Al was walking back to the house squat that he had shared with Doreen.

Al turned to see PJ, Doreen's former boyfriend, crossing the road towards them.

"What the fuck are you doing here?" Doreen cried out.

"I missed you and our daughter," PJ said as a single tear rolled down his cheek. "I've been looking all over Kings Cross for you."

"Well now you've seen me, you can fuck off back to Glasgow!"

"Please, Doreen, I love you and our daughter."

Al could see that PJ's heart was breaking.

"You lied to me," Doreen blurted out, while stabbing her finger towards him. "You promised me a house, furniture, car and holidays but you were all talk and no action."

"I was trying."

"Trying? You did fuck all but serve beer and talk utter bollocks."

"I just need another chance."

"You have no fucking chance. You're a waste of space and there is no room for you in my life."

"Fuck me you're merciless," Al thought as he watched the tears stream down PJ's face.

"I can change," PJ pleaded.

"That's it," Doreen yelled, putting her hands firmly on her hips. "I've wasted enough breath on you!"

PJ lowered his head.

"I'm feeling for you PJ," Al thought.

Doreen turned to Al.

"I'll see you later, and you, PJ," Doreen hissed through gritted teeth. "Don't you dare follow me."

Al and PJ watched as Doreen stomped across the street.

"Can't you do something Al?" PJ whimpered. "I love Doreen and I miss my daughter."

Al shook his head slowly.

"In Doreen's mind you had your chance and you've blown it."

"But..."

"I'm not saying that I agree with her, but you must know that Doreen is determined to get ahead at all costs."

"I know, Al, but my daughter... She took my daughter without a single word."

Al shrugged his shoulders.

"I have never met anyone in my whole life as mercenary as Doreen," Al thought.

"How on earth did you find us?"

"I figured that Doreen would probably come to you and after some asking about I found out that you were in Kings Cross."

"Kings Cross is a big place!"

"Yeah, I know. I've literally gone from one squat to another and searched through every room to find something that led me to Doreen or you."

"How long have you been down here?"

"Six days," PJ said, wiping the tears from his face. "On day three I was searching this big old house and one of the rooms and been used as a toilet."

Al winced.

"When I saw playing cards sticking out of the turds, I figured that to be your sense of humour, so I've been hanging around here ever since, hoping to catch up with either you or Doreen."

"I really need to stop doing that," Al thought.

"What should I do?"

"You don't have any choice," Al said calmly. "You and my sister are done. The best thing you can do is get yourself back to Glasgow and just get on with your life."

"But my daughter, Al, I need to see my daughter."

"This is fucking heart breaking," Al thought.

"Look, just get yourself back to Glasgow and maybe, just maybe, Doreen will take some time out and reflect on what she's done and how it must feel for you not seeing your daughter."

"Do you think so?"

"Not a chance in hell," Al thought.

"You never know, PJ, she could do."

"Yeah," PJ said as he straightened himself up. "If I sort myself out and get on with all the things we talked about, maybe Doreen will have a change of heart and come back to me with my daughter."

Al smiled awkwardly.

"We could be a proper family again."

"How are you for money?" Al said as he reached for his trouser pocket.

"I'm alright Al, thank you."

Al watched as PJ traipsed away with his head down and hands in his pockets.

"Poor fucker." Al thought as PJ turned the street corner.

Al caught up with Doreen, but he knew better than to try and make a case for PJ as he knew it would fall on deaf ears. Once Doreen had made up her mind about a relationship there would be no change. Doreen told Al that she had dumped Leeds, as he too, like Tommy before him, had started to use the heroin he was dealing.

"I've seen it all before with Tommy," Doreen had said. "When you start using, the whole business goes shit shaped and I'm not hanging around and wasting any more of my time with Leeds."

Leeds was to become an addict. He took up with another user, also an addict. Her name was Tessa and she was wheelchair bound. They used the downstairs of a squat as their home.

Al left Doreen and stopped by the Bell pub. He found it was packed with college students celebrating. One group of lads by the bar were urging their friend to do this party trick. The drunken lad kicked off his shoes, bent down and removed his socks before standing upright and smashing an empty bottle of light ale he picked up from the bar, onto the floor. It smashed into small pieces. Al was up and out of his seat in time to see the drunk, surrounded by his friends, dancing in his bare feet on the broken shards of glass to *'Three Minute Hero'* by the Selecter. Once the song had come to an end, Al stepped in and had the lads clean up their mess and told another to take his friend to the hospital for stitches.

Kings Cross was in full swing with money making opportunities presenting themselves at every corner. The streets were filled with working girls who were all keeping busy with sexually starved punters. With no trouble and everyone in good spirits, Al wandered off to the Scottish Stores pub.

The pub was packed with lads out for a good time, girls to provide it, and the criminally active regulars. *'9 to 5'* by Sheena Easton pounded out of the speakers. Despite the packed bar, Duncan, the barman, caught Al's eye and had a tray of lagers and whiskey chasers sent over to his usual table.

"This place is packed," Leaky said as he peered around the pub.

"It's all good for business," Al replied, patting his trouser pocket.

Tammy, Monica and Tanya, a new girl to Kings Cross, were at the adjoining table.

"Al, this is Tanya. She arrived a couple of days ago."

Tanya had a supple, curvaceous figure. Her molten-red hair had been styled and fashioned into a bob that framed her peaches and cream complexion.

"Good to meet you Tanya. This is my friend Leaky. Where are you from?" Al said.

"I'm from Worthing, it's a small town down on the South Coast."

"I told Tanya that she should meet you because you're number one in the Kings Cross."

Al blushed for a moment.

"I have some influence," Al replied. "Are you okay for money?"

"Tammy and Monica have been good to me and shown me the ropes."

"Well done, "Al said as he raised his glass. "It's important that we all stick together in the Cross and help each other wherever possible."

"Thank you," Tanya said.

Al caught the barman's eye, and motioned him to bring a round of drinks for the girls.

"Have you done this kind of work before?" Leaky asked before taking a swig from his drink.

Tanya shook her head.

"I figure if you can do it for a couple of drinks on a night out, then why not make some proper money and set yourself up properly."

"That makes sense," Leaky said.

"You will come across all sorts of needs here," Al said, before rising from the table and walking over to the bar to see a friend about business.

"What you girls do or don't do has nothing to do with me," Al thought. *"It's none of my business."*

"Like what?"

"Oh trust us, you will get some strange requests, but the money will always be good."

"Requests? Like what?" Tanya asked as she turned to Monica.

"I had one guy who just wanted to suck on my feet while he jerked himself off," Monica said. "I rushed him thirty quid for that and he paid up without a quibble."

"Thirty quid!" Tanya said with an astonished expression.

"Yeah, and he didn't touch me."

"I had a punter have me tie him up and leave him in the bathroom with the door locked for a whole hour and he paid me thirty quid too."

"It happens, believe me. I had this nice old fella as a regular a year or so back," Monica said as Duncan placed the tray of drinks on their table. "He liked to watch me open a tin of Ambrosia Creamed

Rice and then jerk himself off while I poured it over his bits dressed in just my bra and panties."

"So it's not just sex, then," Tanya said sheepishly.

"The bulk of your clients will want you to suck them off because they just don't get it at home."

"True."

"While other men, and very occasionally women, will treat themselves to a fantasy."

"Fantasy?"

"Yeah like a threesome; one guy and two girls, or three girls together," Tammy said with a sultry smile. "Monica and I work together. Maybe we could add you to those who are willing to pay for a foursome?"

Monica smiled.

"Guys are always fascinated by redheads."

"Why?"

"They want to know if the cuffs match the collar," Monica said with a smile. "Does it?"

Tanya blushed.

"Yes of course."

"Would you be happy working with another girl?"

Tanya continued to blush.

"I did try it once with an older girl who worked at the same horse stables as me."

"Did you enjoy the experience?" Leaky asked with a wry smile.

Tanya nodded awkwardly.

"Then you'll make a fortune here in the Cross," Leaky said with a raucous laugh.

"What you have to do is decide what you will and won't do, and then put a price on it. Monica and I make good money from the threesomes and most punters will make it a monthly treat for themselves."

"Okay," Tanya said, still blushing.

"Al has a couple of spielers," Leaky said as he leant back into his chair. "If you bring punters in there to drink, you'll also get a cut from the drink sales."

"It's a nice earner and safe," Tammy said.

"The girls will give you the details and should you decide to go, then just say you're friends with Leaky."

As Al walked back to the table his eyes were drawn to a blonde by the bar.

"Here, Leaky, isn't that Margaret over there?"

"Who?"

"Margaret, you know, the girl that is supposed to be with Jackie O'Docherty."

"Where?"

"Over there by the bar with a guy with long grey curly hair wearing a trench coat."

Leaky looked around the busy pub until his eyes rested on the far end of the bustling bar.

"Yeah, that's her," Leaky said.

"That's going to be trouble for someone," Al thought as he turned back towards the girls.

"She's off," Leaky said, motioning Al to look over at the door.

The man in the trench coat helped Margaret with her jacket before opening the door.

"Have you ever seen that fella before?"

"He's not from around here," Leaky said. "He sticks out like a sore thumb."

"Oh shit," Al thought as he watched Shelley walk through the pub doors.

Al had met Shelley a few months earlier and had a five day fling with her.

Shelley had a one-night stand with Butch Jo, a lesbian sex worker, who was later murdered. Butch Jo always dressed in blue jeans with a black leather biker jacket covered in chains. She had short cropped jet black hair that had been shaved around her ears. Butch Jo had approached Al on the street and questioned whether he really needed another notch on his bed post. Al's retort was blunt.

He told Butch Jo that her liaison, as he understood it, was just a one-night stand. Butch Jo wasn't happy, but left.

Shelley had become extremely agitated with Al after he dropped her. She believed that she had given herself for five days because Al was in love with her. Al confessed that he never stayed with any girl for more than a night and so she had been special, but that time had passed. Shelley refused to let it go and would try to argue with him on the streets when they passed. She had, on one occasion, accused him of using and abusing her and threatened to bring her four brothers down to sort him out. Al said that she really shouldn't do that. Shelley, initially, took that as fear. Al continued to say that he didn't want to hospitalise any of her family because she couldn't accept that what they shared had now passed.

A few weeks later, Butch Jo's body was found. A team of overly ambitious truncheon wielding police officers battered Al to the ground before taking him into the police station. Al was taken down to the cells and ritually beaten, then had his head thrust down the toilet and held under water until he choked. He was taken up to the interview rooms where he discovered that they were trying to pin the murder of the prostitute, Butch Jo, on him.

Butch Jo had been suffocated with a plastic bag. Al denied it and was once again returned to the cells where he was kicked, punched and battered. After the ritual beating, he was taken back to the interview rooms where the officers had tried to coerce him into signing a confession by saying that Butch Jo was just a whore and the jury wouldn't care about her death. They promised to put a good word in with the judge and he could probably walk away with a two year sentence. Al knew that they were liars and had no sway with any judge, let alone determining what the prison sentence would be. Al was innocent of the crime and stayed quiet. The Metropolitan police held him for five days without contact with the outside world or food and water. He had been forced to drink the water at the bottom of the toilet bowl.

***

Eventually two prostitutes came forward and made statements. They told the police that Butch Jo had a client who paid well for his kink. Finally, a police officer confessed to the murder. He lusted for erotic asphyxiation play. The officer took immense sexual gratification from intentionally cutting off the girl's air supply to induce choking and suffocating. He confessed that the dominance of breath play had heightened his sexual arousal and made his orgasms far more intense. The officer got off by knowing that the activity carried significant risk and could lead to cardiac arrest and brain damage due to the lack of oxygen. He panicked when Butch Jo died and hid her body under the floorboards, but struggled with the guilt of what had happened.

Butch Jo, for a price, had readily engaged in the submissive power play to satisfy his kinky desires.

The cell doors were finally opened and Al was set free with the custody sergeant telling him that he was one lucky bastard, because every copper in the station wanted it to be him. Al managed to get himself to the hospital where he was x-rayed. In addition to the extensive bodily bruising, Al had suffered multiple fractures to his ribs, arms and legs.

It wasn't that Al was so tough that he sucked up the brutal violence inflicted on him during the incarceration, he was more afraid of going to prison than anything the police officers could possibly do.

The guilty police officer was sentenced to five years. Al vowed to himself that he would mark the bastard for what he did to Butch Jo should their paths ever cross on the inside.

Almost a month had gone by without Al bumping into Shelley.

"There goes trouble," Leaky said with a chuckle

"Tell me about it," Al said. "I'd laugh, but it just isn't funny."

"I told you she was bad news."

Al watched her strut through the bar to a thief he knew that specialised in smash and grab raids.

The pub door flew open and Tottenham Mick bolted across the bar to Al's table.

"Jackie's been shot!"

Al jumped out of his seat. Tottenham Mick told him where the incident had happened before racing across the bar, ripping open the door and running down the Caledonian Road. Without any thought to why he was running to the incident, Al ran to Pollard House.

Pollard House was a squat that was also being used as a brothel.

Al slammed the door open and bolted up the stairs. Amongst the working girls at the party were his friends Kevin Doors, Johnny King, Vodka Pat and Bobby O'Neil. Al pushed through to find Jackie lying on the floor with Margaret leaning over him.

"Fuck me his face is almost white," Al thought. *"Still, having Margaret's tits in your face is a good way to go."*

Margaret had arrived at the party with the man she'd been drinking with in the pub. Jackie was already there drinking heavily, flirting, and playing the part of a major villain. To Margaret, the grey curly haired guy was no more than a paying punter, but Jackie became agitated when he saw them together. There was an exchange of words and then a fight broke out. The stranger had pulled out a gun and Jackie ran straight into it. The barrel pressed against his chest and over his heart. The stranger pulled the trigger and Jackie immediately fell to the floor and in all the commotion the grey curly haired stranger in the trench coat disappeared.

Al took off his jacket, dropped down to his knees and placed it under Jackie's head.

"I love you Jackie," Margaret blurted through the tears.

"He's dying." Al thought as he witnessed the colour slowly leaving his face.

"I love you so much Jackie," Margaret continued.

The door flew open and three uniformed police officers barged in.

"Alright step back, step back."

The crowd around Jackie's body dispersed but Margaret remained firm with uncontrollable tears streaming down her cheeks.

"Can you please give us some room," the officer said.

Margaret shook Jackie's head about like a rag doll

"He's my Jackie and I love him!"

The officer placed his hand on her arm but she shook it off.

"He needs me."

"Let them check him over," one of the working girls called out.

Reluctantly Margaret withdrew.

Jackie O'Docherty was dead.

Moments later two paramedics arrived

The lead officer turned to Al.

"You're with us."

"Why? I haven't done fuck all."

"Al hasn't done anything," Johnny King called out.

"Leave him alone."

"You've got the wrong geezer!"

"I'm sure Mr Al McIntosh won't mind just coming to the station and answering a few questions.

"If I kick off it'll look like I'm guilty," Al thought.

Al was led from Pollard House to the waiting police car where he was whisked off to the police station. Al had expected to be interviewed, but he was taken straight to a cell.

As Al lay back on the prison bed he thought about the conversation that he'd had with Jackie earlier that day. They had been having a drink with two girls and Al had suggested they move on to another pub and try their luck with the girls. Jackie had been reluctant which would have left Al with two girls and certainly killed any hopes for any adventurous liaison.

"If he had come with me he'd still be alive," Al thought.

One full day later Al was taken up to the interview rooms where he was questioned about Jackie O'Docherty's murder. The police, however, didn't believe his version of events and had him returned to the cells.

Al was denied access to a solicitor or any contact with his friends for five days. The police rationale for keeping Al locked away was that 79% of murders are carried out by friends, loved ones or family. They would not entertain that a known face like Jackie O'Docherty could be murdered by a complete stranger.

Margaret confirmed that Jackie had a jealous rage and attacked the stranger. Kevin Doors, Johnny King, Vodka Pat, Tottenham Mick, Bobby 'O'Neil and most of the girls at the party gave statements backing up Al's story. After Big William and several others from the pub gave statements confirming that Al was not at the party, they finally let him leave without charge.

A senior police officer stopped Al at the exit.

"We've been hearing all about your escapades in Kings Cross, Al McIntosh, and if you think you can get away with organised crime on our patch, you're very wrong. Mark my words... we are coming for you."

Chapter 10

Al was having a drink with a couple of hookers he knew at a brothel just outside of Kings Cross.

"We haven't seen you in ages," Shirley said.

Shirley had escaped an abusive relationship in Scotland. She travelled down to Kings Cross after reading about the 'Away Day Girls' in the Sun Newspaper. She was a pretty girl with a positive attitude which allowed to her to integrate into the Kings Cross culture quickly. She had moved from working the street corners during the Leicester mob conflict, to working within a brothel. It saved her standing out in the cold, working in stranger's cars, and was safer because the brothel employed a minder, Lenny, who Al had recommended to the House Madam.

"I've been busy," Al said with a chuckle.

"We heard that you'd fallen for a Turkish girl," Mandy said.

Mandy had been working the Lanes down in Brighton. Business had been good during the summer periods with holiday makers and day trippers looking for a special memory. However, during the winter months, business was scarce and the monthly bills soon caught up with her illicit income. The Sun newspaper article had registered as a potential plan B. One Friday morning she clambered out of bed, took a look out of her window at the empty streets and decided to invest in a ticket to Kings Cross and trial working there. Mandy was making more money in a week than she did working a full month during the summer. She met Shirley while working the Sutton Arms in Caledonian Road.

The Sutton Arms pub was owned by a famous celebrity and his friend. The pub would host private lesbian shows for punters and the girls were all supplied by Black Sandra.

"Nah, I'm not the one girl type," Al said before sipping his whiskey. "You have to keep your options open."

"That's what I said."

"It did sound as if she'd captured your heart," Shirley said.

Al shook his head.

"How is Lenny getting on?"

"Oh he's lovely," Mandy said with a wry smile.

"Has there been any trouble here I should know about?"

Shirley shook her head.

"Business is good, no problems with punters or the old bill."

"Good," Al said before drinking the last of his whiskey.

Suddenly the front door was kicked in and there stood Jimmy Connelly with a rifle.

"You're fucking dead now!" Jimmy Connelly yelled out.

Both Shirley and Mandy screamed and bolted towards the hallway door as Jimmy Connelly pulled the trigger.

Bang!

Al heard the bullet whistle past his head and hit the wall behind him.

BANG!

The second bullet missed and lodged in the wall too.

Al clenched his fists and let out a terrifying war cry as he bolted towards Jimmy Connelly. Jimmy tried desperately to fire again, but failed. Al grabbed an old wooden wardrobe and pulled it down on Jimmy. He dropped the rifle and fell to the floor under the weight of the wardrobe. Al clambered on top of the wardrobe and began to jump up and down. Jimmy cried out as the solid timber crushed his body, but Al continued to jump up and stamp down with all the strength he could muster. Little by little the wardrobe creaked, splintered and broke on top of Jimmy. With the wardrobe now in broken pieces and Jimmy lying motionless, Al finally stopped.

As the adrenaline rush wore off, Al stepped back and looked down at Jimmy.

"Urgh," Jimmy whimpered.

"If you ever come here again, I'll put you in the ground," Al hissed before sending one final kick into a part of Jimmy's body that wasn't covered in broken wood.

Al left the brothel and walked towards Kings Cross. As his anger subsided, it was replaced by an agonising pain. Both his legs were covered with hundreds of deep wooden splinters

"What a liberty!" Al thought as he visualised Jimmy standing in the doorway taking aim with his rifle. *"I should have finished that bastard. First he puts a contract out on me, and now this. If I didn't have all this bollocks with the bouncers hanging over me, I'd end Jimmy Connelly."*

A few months earlier Al had met up with his friend, Limerick Mick, who had just done a short spell in prison. They had agreed to meet at the Green Man on the Euston Road to have a few drinks and celebrate his release. Al was wearing all his new clothes and had over five hundred pounds in his pocket. He was feeling great and ready to party. No sooner were they in the pub and downing a couple of drinks than a couple of working girls joined them.

The Green Man had two black bouncers to mind the doors and keep rowdy drinkers in check. One of the lads was heavy set and stood a good six foot two inches, while his shorter colleague measured around five foot ten. They were both dressed in black suits, white shirts and highly polished shoes. Both Al and Limerick Mick had ignored them on entry and went straight to the bar to start their party. With the drinks flowing, the girls giggling, and the pub's punters gravitating towards the party, the two doormen had ventured inside. Al noticed that the larger of the two bouncers had passed them twice. Al took out a wad of pound notes and placed them on the table.

"What is he fucking look at?" Limerick Mick said as the shorter bouncer passed their table for the third time.

"Ignore him," Al said, as he handed one of the girls a bundle of notes and asked her to get another round in.

Al could see the two bouncers talking amongst themselves and then looking over at their table.

"That big lump is getting on my tits," Limerick Mick whispered.

Moments later the two bouncers strode slowly towards the table.

Limerick Mick looked straight up at the larger of the two bouncers.

"What is it with you?" Limerick Mick hissed. "Do you fancy me or something? What, do you want to get up me?"

The larger of the two bouncers took a single step closer to the table.

"Don't you know who we are?"

"Oh here we go again," Al thought as he clenched his fists below the table. *"How many times do I have to hear that?"*

"Listen lads," Al said calmly. "My friend and I are out to have a good night. We're wedged up with plenty of money and spending in this pub, so what is your problem?"

The bouncers both just stood by the table.

"We're not looking for any trouble, so my advice to you is to just walk away," Al said.

Limerick Mick finished his pint.

The larger of the bouncers stood upright and thrust his chest out to exaggerate his size.

"I'm afraid you two will have to leave."

Limerick Mick was out of his chair and threw a calamitous right hander at the larger bouncer. The shorter bouncer pulled out a blade and sunk it into Limerick Mick's leg.

"Argghh," Limerick Mick cried out.

As Al rose from his chair, the larger bouncer grabbed a wooden chair and brought it crashing down on his head.

"Now you're done!" Al thought as he shoved the table to one side and weighed in with a heavy barrage of quick firing left and right handers.

The larger bouncer tripped and fell backwards. Al looked down at the knife sticking out of Limerick Mick's leg before launching a vigorous kick that caught the shorter bouncer right between the legs. He yelped, grabbed his crotch, and fell to his knees. Al reached over and helped Limerick Mick onto his feet. He helped him through the busy pub with the knife still sticking out of his leg. The pub's patrons parted as they made their way to the door. Once outside, Al could hear the sound of distant police sirens.

"Come on mate we have to get out of here," Al said as they scuttled down the street.

"My fucking leg is killing me," Limerick Mick bleated as Al turned into an alleyway and off the main road.

"Come on, we don't want to get nicked!" Al said as he dragged his friend down the dark alleyway.

Al looked up at the wall and then back to the road.

"The old bill will be here in no time," Al said. "We've got to get over this wall."

The top of the wall was covered with glass that had been cemented in to keep people out. Al rested Limerick against the wall before taking off his leather jacket and placing it over the glass.

"That should do it," Al thought as he grappled with Limerick Mick.

"Leave me here," Limerick said. "Or we'll both get nicked."

"We're both getting out of here," Al said as he turned Limerick Mick towards the wall and cupped his hands under Limericks Mick's right foot.

"Right, now push!" Al said.

Limerick Mick used all his strength to clamber up onto to the wall as a police car raced by with its light flashing.

Limerick Mick was on the wall and then managed to climb down the other side.

"Stop!"

Al turned to see a figure racing towards him.

"It's that fucking bouncer," Al thought before turning sharply and delivering a punch that had the figure flat out on the ground.

Al pulled himself up onto the wall, took one last look down the dark alleyway and then jumped.

SPLASH!

Al had landed in water.

"My leg, my bloody leg!" Al hissed as pain shot through his entire body.

Al tried to wade through the water but couldn't move his leg.

"I can't drown in this," Al thought as panic struck him.

Al tried over and over to move his leg but it wouldn't budge.

The cold, dank, water splashed over his face.

"This is not my time," Al thought as he felt a surge of strength pass down into his hands and arms.

Al managed to grab the bank and wrapped his hands around a metal rod that was sticking out of the ground. He closed his eyes, summoned all his strength, and pulled.

"Arghhhhh" Al hissed through gritted teeth.

Al could feel his leg slowly moving.

"Arghhh," he hissed again as his leg was back within his control.

Al reached up to the water bank and tugged on the metal bar and the branch of a nearby bush until he had pulled himself out of the water. He looked down at his leg and found a child's tricycle had embedded itself.

"Oh no, no, no," Al thought as he pulled himself up onto his feet and began slowly trudging down the embankment using the wall as a guide.

Limerick Mick had long gone.

It took Al over an hour to find an opening in the wall. He was soaked through to the skin and the pain from his injured leg was excruciating. He managed to flag down a taxi driver who was hesitant at first about taking the fare. Al peeled off one hundred pounds to take him to a prostitute he knew in Islington.

Fortunately Lindy wasn't working, and quickly, Al, along with the kiddie's tricycle still stuck in his leg, was inside her private flat. She took his wet clothes off and made him comfortable before calling one of her regular clients, a doctor. At first the doctor didn't want to help, but Lindy threatened to tell his wife that she had been fucking her husband every Tuesday and Thursday afternoon for the last twelve months.

The doctor arrived within twenty minutes and proceeded to sedate Al and remove the tricycle. He cleaned and stitched the wound. Al asked Lindy to give him a hundred pounds from his trouser pocket.

Al could hear the doctor and Lindy having stern words in the hallway before he left. She assured Al that she would win the doctor back over by performing a couple of his guilty pleasures. Lindy made up a bed and Al stayed there until the following morning.

Al had only been in the Bell for a few minutes before the police came crashing in and arrested him for Grievous Bodily Harm. He later learnt that the figure in the alleyway that he had clumped was not one of the bouncers, but a police officer attempting to make an arrest. In his rush to get away, Al had left his leather jacket on the wall. They were able to take finger prints from the articles in his pockets and also found an envelope, which they claimed was empty but in fact had several hundred pounds in it, that read:

A little something to help you get back on your feet

Al

Al was brought before a magistrate the following morning and was shocked when he was granted bail.

Limerick Mick went on the run and later called the Scottish Stores from Dublin to say that he was safe. *"I can't be doing with any attention right now,"* Al thought. *"Jimmy Connelly you're a slag!"*

"Al, hello mate."

AL was brought back to reality when he turned to see Albert McInnerney.

"You looked miles away," Albert said with a broad smile.

"I was," Al replied.

"Here, how do you fancy doing another KFC run for a laugh?"

Albert McInnerney was a great practical joker and enjoyed playing pranks. On one occasion he had talked Al into going into the Kentucky Fried Chicken shop with him. They ordered two bargain buckets and when they were placed on the counter, both Al and Albert grabbed a bucket of finger licking chicken, bolted out of the door, and ran wildly down the road laughing their heads off while taking big bites of the deep fried chicken with eleven herbs and spices.

Al found himself smiling as the memory came back.

"I can't at the moment."

"Another time then?"

"Yeah, maybe."

"Al, can I talk to you about Doreen?"

"Depends."

"I really like her Al."

"Here we go again," Al thought. *"What is it with all these blokes and my sister?"*

"So ask her out then."

"I did and she said no."

"That's because you've got nothing to offer," Al thought.

Albert was a great joker and everybody around the Cross enjoyed his company until he had that one drink too many. It was then that he could become loud and obnoxious.

"I was hoping that you'd put in a good word for me."

Al chuckled.

"Believe me when I tell you that no one, and I do mean no one, has any sway with my sister."

"Come on Al, I really need your help."

"I can't tell you about my sister, but I can tell you what I do to get a girl's attention."

Albert beamed.

"Be funny but don't be crude, that never goes down well. You're a funny fella so you already have that working for you. Everybody likes a good laugh and if you can get a girl's attention by being funny then you're making headway."

"You mean like jokes and stuff?"

Al shook his head.

"It's important to figure out what kind of humour you think will work, but I'd say with Doreen, like most girls, use quick witty humour. If she thinks it's funny, she'll laugh. Situational wit almost always goes down well; see something or someone do something and make a joke from it."

"Okay."

"Taking the piss out of someone never goes down well and will kill any chance you've ever had."

"Noted."

"Taking the piss out of yourself and a situation you were in is always a safe bet."

"I should be bleeding well charging for this," Al thought

"Show passion for whatever it is you do, girls like that."

"I'm a thief," Albert said, shrugging his shoulders.

"So be excited about how you plan out what you do, then how you executed your plan and finally what you did with all the proceeds. If you have to be a thief then be the best, and make it appear that in the world of thieves, you're the number one."

"I can do that."

"Good."

"Girls just don't like men that strut around with their chests stuck out playing the hard man."

"Don't they?"

"You have to show girls that you have emotional depth and that there's more to you than everyone else sees."

Albert nodded enthusiastically.

"Show them empathy and that you can relate to how others are feeling."

"This is good stuff."

"It's how I am, not what I try to do to get laid," Al thought.

"Most girls, and this includes Doreen, like men that are polite and courteous. Whatever you do, don't go saying or doing things that people consider offensive and that includes swearing, and making racist or sexist jokes. They are a big turn off."

Albert continued to nod enthusiastically.

"Remember that just because the boys around the pub might find one thing funny, that doesn't mean that it'll go down well with the girls."

"Got it."

"Finally, to win a girl like Doreen over, you will need to have ambition and a strong sense of adventure."

"Thanks Al," Albert said.

"No problem. Now mate, I have to make tracks. I've got some business to attend to."

"Cheers, Al, see you later."

Al continued to walk down towards Kings Cross when he spotted someone he hadn't seen in a while.

"Leeds, is that you?"

Al spotted Leeds, Doreen's ex-boyfriend, standing by the entrance to an alleyway.

"Hello Al, you alright?

Al crossed the road towards him.

"I'm sorry to hear about you and Doreen," Al said as he joined Leeds on the pavement.

"You look a mess!" Al thought as he noticed Leeds' scruffy appearance.

Leeds drug business had allowed him to wear good quality clothes, have his hair styled and his nails manicured. He had taken pride in his appearance which was how he attracted the beautiful Doreen.

"Fuck me, you smell a bit ripe too," Al thought as he took a short step back.

"It happens," Leeds said as he shrugged his shoulders. "Do you fancy getting sucked off?"

"What?"

"Tessa will suck you off for a tenner," Leeds said. "She'll swallow it all too."

"Who is Tessa?"

"My girlfriend," Leeds said, rubbing his hands together. "She's in the alleyway."

Al took several steps to his right and peered up the alleyway where he made out a girl in a wheelchair sucking off some punter's penis.

"What the fuck are you playing at?" Al said sternly. "You're pimping a girl in a wheelchair out for sex with strangers."

"We need the money for gear," Leeds replied.

"You need to slow down and let that sink in," Al continued. "If the police catch you pimping out a disabled girl, what the fuck do you think they'll do to you?"

"I know, I know," Leeds said as his eyes became teary.

"They will kick seven shades of shit out of you and the judge will lock you up and throw away the key!"

"We don't want to be doing this," Leeds pleaded before bursting into tears. "It's the heroin... it's got us and when it calls we need to do whatever we can to get the ten pound bag."

"You need to get yourselves sorted out because this can only end in two ways," Al said firmly. "Either you'll end up banged up for a long time or you'll be found dead in a squat with a needle hanging out of your arm."

The tears streamed down Leeds' face as he began to cry uncontrollably.

"I can't even give them a few quid to help them out," Al thought. *"Because they'll just shoot it up."*

Leeds fell to his knees, rested his face between his hands, and cried.

Al spotted the punter leaving the alleyway look towards him briefly, before scampering off.

"Go on, fuck off, you sick bastard," Al thought as he scowled.

Drug users who develop the habit and become addicts can, once they've exhausted relationships with family and friends, turn to crime to feed their insatiable habit. While casual criminals will accelerate and extend their criminal activities

Leeds promised Al that he would wheel Tessa to the hospital and seek help for their addiction.

"How can a guy who appeared to have it all together fall so far?" Al thought as he continued his journey. *"Leeds was no mug; he battered Balkan Bill and stabbed him with a screwdriver for pushing his luck and being disrespectful."*

***

A few days later Al was sat at his usual table at the Scottish Stores pub. It was just after mid-day when the barman, Duncan, placed the first pint in front of him. As he sipped at his pint, he made a mental list of things he had to do that day.

The doors of the pub opened and four serious looking men walked in.

"This looks like trouble," Al thought as he weighed them up. *"That's the South London firm."*

The leader turned towards Al, smiled, and led his muscle-bound entourage over.

"Al McIntosh?"

"That would be me." Al said calmly.

"Do you know who I am?"

Al nodded.

"Good, that will save us both time," the leader said before pulling up a chair and facing Al.

"What do you want?"

"Firm and direct... I like that approach, so let me be the same."

Al looked down at his drink and chose to leave it there.

"You've had an altercation with an associate of ours."

"Okay."

"Who the fuck is he on about?" Al thought while remaining calm.

"Jimmy Connelly."

Al sighed, shook his head and began to chuckle.

"Do you find this funny?"

Al went on to explain to the South London Boss that he did indeed know Jimmy Connelly, and that his nineteen-year-old daughter had come on to him. Jimmy had become agitated when his daughter kicked back and told him that she'll do what she wants, when she wants and with whom ever she wants and that it was none of his business. Jimmy sought out a hit man and took out a contract on him for the princely sum of four thousand pounds. However, the hit man had a relationship with Al and shared the bounty, which must have agitated Jimmy further because he turned up at a friend's brothel yelling and screaming. He had a rifle and took two shots at him. Al told the South London Firm's boss that he beat the shit out of Jimmy and on reflection should have finished the job and taken him out."

"Jimmy didn't mention any of this," the mob boss said.

148

"He wouldn't though, would he?" Al said with a half-smile.

"According to Jimmy you've been pestering his daughter and he wanted us to teach you a lesson; you know, break a few bones. Just give you a little something to think about."

There was a moment's silence.

"I think Jimmy may have been lying to us." The mob boss said as he turned to the men standing behind him.

They nodded.

"Well we're sorry to have bothered you, Al McIntosh," the mob boss said as he stood up. "You're an interesting fella and I'm pleased that we've met."

Al reached out and shook the mob boss's hand.

"We'll be having a word with Jimmy Connelly."

Al heard, through associates, that the South London Firm had gone straight to Jimmy Connelly's house and given him a good talking to before taking his brand new Ford Cortina Ghia as compensation.

PHOTOGRAPHS

The Bell Pub in Kings Cross

The Scottish Stores Pub in Kings Cross

The Old Bailey - the Central Criminal Court for England & Wales

Justice statue above the roof of the Old Bailey

A courtroom

A prison landing

Chapter 11

It was still early when Al passed through Kings Cross and spotted Leeds standing by the alleyway talking to what was clearly a punter.

"He's at it again," Al thought as he watched the punter hand over money and disappear up the alley. *"You're the lowest of the low."*

Al continued his stroll down to a café by Kings Cross station where he met with Leaky. The two men ordered a full English breakfast and strong, hot, tea.

"We may have trouble," Leaky said as he cut into the pork sausage.

"What's up?"

"Vodka Pat was nicked yesterday.

"Shit!" Al said, putting his knife and fork down.

Vodka Pat was a major supplier of stolen credit cards. She would use brake fluid to remove the signature and then sell them on. The recipients could then sign the stolen card themselves and use up all the credit. Vodka Pat had earned her nickname because she drank, on average, three full bottles of vodka every day. She had a turbulent relationship with her black boyfriend from Brixton. On one occasion during an argument, the boyfriend had produced a decorator's knife and sliced open her cheek. She managed to get to hospital and have the wound sewn up, but she was scarred for life. Al believed that it was the scar that made her increase her drinking from one bottle of vodka to three.

"What happened?"

"From what I've been told, Vodka Pat was out of her mind drunk, she stripped off and then traipsed off down the shops, stark bollock naked, and bought three bottles of Vodka. As you can imagine, seeing her like that caused a bit of a stir and somebody has called the old bill."

"Bloody drink and drugs," Al thought. *"Buggers up good business."*

"Well Vodka Pat has drunk the bloody lot and is sprawled out unconscious on the bed. She's only gone and left the door open and the old bill have swooped in and found all the credit cards."

"Is she talking?"

"Not a word."

"You're right, this could be a problem," Al said as he picked up his cutlery and cut into his bacon.

"The old bill is talking about a hundred grand plus in cards that were taken."

"That was our pay day," Al thought as he ate the bacon.

As Al popped the last of his fried bread into his mouth, he spotted Doreen pass by the window.

"Doreen!" Al called out.

Doreen turned, smiled, and came into the café.

Al immediately noticed that she had bruises on her face and arms.

"What happened to you?"

"Albert McInnerney did it."

"Did what?" Al asked as the anger began to build in his stomach.

Leaky motioned the young girl behind the counter to bring over three teas.

"Albert was in need of a place to stay, so I reluctantly agreed. He paid and could be good company sometimes."

"Right," Al said motioning her to continue.

"Well it was all going okay until one night and we've both had a couple of drinks."

"But you're pregnant," Al thought.

"Well Albert has started trying it on and I've let him know that it was never going to happen."

Leaky pushed the teas in front of Al and Doreen.

"We carried on drinking and Albert has tried it on again, and this time I was a bit firmer and pushed him away," Doreen said before blowing the steam off her tea. "Albert has gone mental and he's grabbed me. I fought back, but he's just thrown me across the room and I've gone straight down the stairs."

"He threw you down the stairs?"

Doreen nodded.

"I'll be having a word."

"Leave it Al," Doreen said. "It should never have happened."

"Fucking right it shouldn't have happened, and not to my sister!" Al thought as he clenched and unclenched his fists.

"He was sorry," Doreen said. "He didn't mean for it to happen."

Al closed his eyes and gently released his tightened fists.

"Are you hungry?"

Doreen nodded.

After breakfast Al ventured off to meet with Toprak for an afternoon of adventurous sex at their usual hotel meeting place. It was to be the last time they would meet. Al sensed that the magnetism between them was wearing thin, and with so many available girls in and around the Kings Cross area, he was content that the relationship was coming to a close. Al suspected that her womanising husband had warned her off him or she had met someone else to continue her open marriage adventure with.

Al decided to have a drink at the Sutton Arms on the Caledonian Road in Islington. The select clientele would be treated to a regular lesbian show. All the girls for the venue were supplied by Black Sandra. Al walked through the doors and immediately surveyed the pub and saw Albert McInnerney sitting with his sister Doreen.

Al felt a bolt of anger wash over his entire body.

"That bastard threw my pregnant sister down the stairs!" Al thought while ordering two double whiskeys.

Al drank the first in one shot and then turned to see Albert and Doreen happily engaging in conversation.

"I don't like blokes that hit women, and I take exception to anyone laying a hand on my sister," Al thought before downing the second whiskey.

Al ordered two more double whiskeys.

"Being drunk is no excuse," Al thought as he watched his sister laughing with Albert.

Al looked down at his watch.

"I could finish this and catch up with Leaky at the Scottish Stores," Al thought while sipping his drink.

A second wave of intense anger washed over him.

"I can't let this go!" Al thought as he swallowed both his drinks and strutted over to the table where Doreen and Albert were sitting.

Al could feel the rage brewing in his stomach as Albert looked up at him.

"Why the fuck are you sitting with him?" Al said.

"Just leave it Al," Doreen said calmly.

"Have a drink Al," Albert said.

Al's eyebrows lowered into a scowl.

"It was an accident Al," Doreen pleaded.

"Like fuck it was!"

From the corner of his eye he could see Albert downing his drink. He sat upright and pushed his shoulders back while forcing his chest out.

"If you're not going to have a drink with us then just fuck the hell off!" Albert hissed, maintaining firm eye contact with Al.

"What did you just say?"

"You heard me."

"You and me, outside," Al said before turning swiftly on his heels and striding towards the pub door.

Once outside on the street, Al adopted his usual fighting stance by spreading his feet out to the same width as his shoulders. He bent both knees with his left leg positioned slightly forward.

"It's about time someone put you on your back!" Albert shouted before throwing a left hook.

Al sidestepped the punch and launched a powerful right hander that shook his opponent. Albert shook his head and raised both his fists to protect his face.

"I fucking eat woman beaters like you for breakfast," Al thought as he fired one potent strike after another. Al glanced down and saw his opening. He fired a final left hook before rapidly stepping back and propelling his right foot straight between Albert's legs.

"Arghh!" Albert cried out before dropping to his knees and cupping his groin.

"If you ever touch my sister again I'll fucking kill you!"

Albert reached into his right hand pocket and pulled out a six inch stainless blade.

"You're done McIntosh!" Albert said as he clambered back onto his feet and began stabbing and slashing wildly.

An intense rage powered up from Al's stomach while adrenaline raced furiously through his body. Al's senses were heightened. A wild stab narrowly missed him.

SMACK! SMACK! SMACK!

Al powered one almighty punch after another in rapid succession. As Albert soaked up the punches he staggered backwards and dropped the knife. Al stepped back, crouched down and picked up the blade. With his hand wrapped firmly around the blade's handle he relentlessly punched and kicked Albert until he fell, beaten, onto the path. As Albert turned away Al sunk the blade into his face.

"Arghhhhh!"

Al looked down at the blood on his hands and the six inch knife stuck in the side of Albert McInnerney's face. He clambered up onto his feet and rubbed his blood soaked hands onto his jeans.

"Yes!" Al shouted as he stood over his victim.

Al took a quick look around him before racing off down the Caledonian Road.

"He had that coming!" Al thought as he walked at pace. *"Pulling a knife on me, he had to have it."*

A blue Rover P6 hooted as Al crossed the road.

"I had no choice," Al thought as the adrenaline wore off along with the fury that had demanded justice for challenging his Kings Cross status and the attack on his sister. *"If he dies, then fuck him."*

Al had been arrested several times for savage, violent, conflicts and on each occasion the victim had either dropped the charges or failed to attend the court hearing. He was confident that this act of violence, providing Albert didn't die, would play out the same way as all the others.

Chapter 12

Duncan, the barman, had just put a tray of drinks on Al's usual table when *'Atomic'* by Blondie played on the jukebox.

"I love this song," Leaky said as he raised his glass. "She's a cracking looking bird too."

"Who?" Brian asked.

"Debbie Harry."

Brian shrugged his shoulders.

"You're kidding me," Leaky said with a quizzical expression. "You must know who Debbie Harry from Blondie is."

Brian took a sip of his lager.

"Brian, she is probably the sexiest looking bird in the charts since…. Suzie Quatro," Leaky said. "Come on, she looks like a Marilyn Monroe with all the curves, lumps and bumps in all the right places."

"I don't watch much television."

"Well then my friend, you're missing out. What do you think Al?"

"Stunning girl," Al said. "She can belt out a good tune too."

"I'd drink her bath water," Leaky said with a raucous laugh.

"You're a sick man," Al said with a chuckle.

The Scottish Stores pub was packed with the usual villains, punters and working girls.

"Is business good?"

Al turned to Leaky.

"The spielers are flying," Al said with a wry smile. "The punters are happy; the girls are earning and I'm coining it. What about you?"

"Bootsie and Smudge have cleared me out of cheque books and giros and the girls are buying my fivers up quicker than I can get them printed. So yes, mate, all is going great," Leaky said as he sat back in his chair.

"Life is so good right now I can fucking taste it," Al thought.

Moments later, just as one of the working girls placed *'Too Much Too Young'* by the Specials on the jukebox, the clear glass by the pub ceiling filled with blue and white flashing lights.

"The police," Brian said calmly.

Leaky kicked his sports bag full of forged five pound notes out from under the table towards the empty table to his left.

"What's all this about?" Al thought as he reached for his lager.

The music continued to play and villains drank, while punters looking for a good night out became uncomfortable around the working girls, as a senior police officer, closely followed by twelve uniformed officers, entered the pub.

The senior officer had a crown badge on his epaulettes, the same as a major in the British army. He was a Metropolitan Superintendent; a rank that was senior to a Chief Inspector, but junior to a Chief Superintendent.

"This is serious," Leaky whispered as the Superintendent looked around the pub before resting his gaze on Al.

The Superintendent ordered a bottle of whiskey from the bar and with two glasses he strode confidently across the bar towards Al's table.

"I'm going to need your seat," the Superintendent said to Leaky.

Al nodded to both Leaky and Brian. Both men rose from their seats and moved to the empty table next to them. The superintendent placed the whiskey and glasses on the table. He opened the bottle and poured two large measures and pushed one towards Al.

Al noticed that one of the police officers had a wooden table leg in his hand. The Superintendent introduced himself to Al.

"So how do you want to do this?"

Al took a short sip of the drink.

"We can do it the hard way or the easy way."

Al looked around at the uniformed officers and then at his friends, business partners and allies around the pub.

"I've got twenty hard core men here and we could batter you lot into next week," Al thought as he sipped the whiskey.

"I don't care how many pals you have here, you are coming with us."

"What, is this over that fucking bouncer incident?" Al thought

Al had been released on bail for an incident with two bouncers while celebrating Limerick Mick's release from jail. It later transpired that the guy he clumped in the dark alleyway was a police officer and not one of the bouncers.

The superintendent swallowed his drink in one go.

"We have accumulated a huge amount of information on you and your activities during the last three weeks. You, Al McIntosh, and your so called pals are all animals!"

Al shrugged his shoulders.

"I suppose you think you've walked away quietly from the Albert McInnerney stabbing?"

"What, he shopped me to the old bill?" Al thought.

"Oh, Albert McInnerney certainly did put your name in the frame, but he wouldn't press charges.

"Phew!" Al thought.

"However, we have a witness."

"Shit!" Al thought, remaining ice cool on the surface.

"We've got you," the Superintendent said, refilling both their glasses.

Al took a moment to let it sink in.

"Animals, you called me and my friends animals," Al said calmly.as he sipped his drink.

"Your behaviour is repellent, revolting and repulsive."

"Really," Al said as he straightened himself in the chair.

The police officers were holding their truncheons.

"So what about you lot, the alleged greatest police force in the world?"

The Superintendent sipped on his whiskey.

"Let's get this straight. The Metropolitan police have been fitting up innocent men, taking bribes and abusing their power for personal gain."

The Superintendent continued to sip on his drink while the officers behind him looked increasingly agitated.

"The Met have sent innocent men to the gallows for crimes by fabricating evidence and lying to juries. Our criminal behaviour may be questionable, but you lot are supposed to represent the law of the land, and yet you have left wives and children without a husband, father and provider. That, to me, is the true definition of a fucking animal, so don't you dare take any moral high ground with me!"

There was a moment's silence as the tension around the pub reached new highs. Both Al and the Superintendent drank their whiskey.

Al placed his empty glass on the table just as *'Ernie (The Fastest Milkman in the West)'* by Benny Hill began to play.

The Superintendent refilled it.

'You could hear the hoof beats pound

As they raced across the ground

And the clatter of the wheels

As they spun round and round'

A smile swept across his face as the 70s song played while he looked around the pub.

"It's over," Al thought. *"My reign* over *the Kings Cross empire has come to an end."*

Brian nodded and held up both clenched fists. Leaky indicated that he was ready while others around the pub were on high alert. The uniformed police officers were outnumbered and no match for the violent men and women of Kings Cross.

Al rose from his chair.

The Scottish Stores pub was deadly silent with just Benny Hill singing the song's chorus *'Ernie and he drove the fastest milk cart in the west'.*

The Superintendent drank the last of his whiskey and wiped his mouth before standing. Al held out both his arms and the Superintendent handcuffed him.

Al was led from the Scottish Stores pub and placed inside a waiting police van. At the police station Al was formally arrested for Grievous Bodily Harm (GBH) and was processed before being taken to the custody sergeant. He was banged up in the police cell overnight. The following morning he was taken before a Magistrate where he was refused bail.

Industrial relations between the government and the Prison Officers Union had broken down with officers being called out on strike. Al was taken to Romford police station where he was held in the cells.

"I didn't need to get into that fight with Albert McInnerney," Al thought as he lay back on his prison bed. *"I had a few drinks and I've seen Albert change and get brave after one too many. He was sorry, Doreen didn't want it to happen, and yet I still weighed in... Al you acted like a fucking mug!"*

The custody sergeant wasn't looking for any trouble and had allowed visits to those that were being held on bail. Black Sandra had tracked Al down and was the first to visit him.

"Hello Al," Black Sandra said as she entered the cell and then threw her arms around him.

"Thanks for visiting me!" Al whispered in her ear before stepping back.

"Everyone was ready to fight your corner," Black Sandra said as she sat down bedside him.

"I know," Al replied. "But it was over and I knew it."

Al told her what his charges were and about the outstanding GBH charge on a police officer during the bouncer incident.

"I was jealous for quite a while," Black Sandra said.

"Jealous? What of?"

"Toprak."

Toprak and her husband owned a Turkish restaurant in Kings Cross and had agreed to an open relationship. Al had been smitten by her good looks, erotic outlook and femininity.

"But we agreed to no expectations or hold on one another."

"I know but she was just so beautiful and I thought for a while, that you would take up with her and maybe leave Kings Cross."

Al chuckled to himself.

"It was just good sex for us both and when it felt like the time to move on came, that's what we both did."

"I didn't want to lose my friend."

"That would never happen," Al said as he placed his arm around her shoulders.

Al and Black Sandra spent a very pleasant couple of hours chatting about memories, exploits and the laughs they had together. The custody sergeant hadn't watched the clock. Black Sandra said she would visit him again.

Chapter 13

Al was transferred from Bow Street Police station, where the officers had spat on Al's food and chastised him, to Highbury Magistrates Court cells.

Being locked up in the holding cells felt like time was moving backwards. There was no association or time out. The sergeant made it very clear that he didn't want them there any more than they wanted to be there, and had shared a couple of tins of lager with Al. The black prisoner opposite Al's cell would regularly hurl abuse and threats at the sergeant.

Al thought that he was a decent enough fella for a copper.

As the sergeant walked down the corridor carrying four tins of lager, the black prisoner smashed his fists against the cell door.

"Come over here and I'll cut your fucking throat!"

"For fuck's sake mate, give it a rest," Al called out.

The sergeant handed two tins of lager to Al.

"I'll smash you both into next week!"

"I don't think so," Al thought, before taking a long swig from the tin.

"Thanks."

"Like I said Al, we can all just get along until the strike is resolved and everything goes back to normal."

Black Sandra was shown through to Al's cell by the sergeant.

"Vodka Pat was found dead."

Al had a soft spot for Vodka Pat. She was the premier supplier of credit cards to London villains, but had nailed her love and loyalties to a lad from Brixton. Their relationship could be volatile and on one occasion the boyfriend slashed Vodka Pat's face with a razor-sharp knife, leaving her scarred for life. They had separated and Vodka Pat began to drink a minimum of three bottles a day until she was arrested with hundreds of thousands of pounds worth of credit cards.

"Was it...?"

"The boyfriend, Darnell?"

"That's the one."

"Yeah, it was him."

"What happened?"

"Vodka Pat was in a bad way," Black Sandra said. "She had the arrest hanging over her and pressure to stay in business. Darnell turned up full of being sorry and in no time he was in the house, in her knickers and her purse. He made lots of promises of a life far away from London where they could be happy, but all the time he was spending her money on drugs and drink. Vodka Pat knew it, but she just kept drinking herself silly until everything came to a climax."

"I never liked that fella," Al thought. *"He was just wrong."*

"Darnell beat her senseless and stabbed her repeatedly before driving her body down to the New Forest where he chopped her up and buried the limbs."

"The bastard!" Al thought.

"A woman out walking her dog found a shallow hole with a limb in it and called the police."

"What about Darnell?"

"The police tracked him down to a squat in Stockwell and nicked him for murder."

"Fucking right," Al hissed as he visualised her body parts being dug up by police officers.

"If I bump into him I'll hurt him good and proper," Al thought.

The police sergeant stood at the cell door.

"Is it time already?" Al asked.

"No," the sergeant said with a wry smile. "I wondered if you'd like some alone time."

Al and Black Sandra looked at each other, smiled and then nodded to the police sergeant.

The cell door was closed and locked. Black Sandra immediately leaped on Al with passionate kisses while tugging frantically at his trousers.

The police sergeant knocked on the door an hour later.

"Is everything okay?"

"Yes, all done," Al called back as he zipped up his trousers.

As the officer opened the cell door, the black prisoner opposite banged aggressively on his door.

"That ain't fucking fair. I ain't getting no booze and no bloody pussy!"

"Maybe you should think about your behaviour," Al said calmly.

"Babylon!"

***

January 2nd 1981.

"We've got him!" the police sergeant cried out.

"Who?" Al replied.

"We've got the Ripper!"

Peter William Sutcliffe had been dubbed in the mainstream press reports as The Yorkshire Ripper. The serial killer had brutally murdered thirteen women, and attempted to murder seven others in and around red-light districts between 1975 and 1980. While driving a vehicle with false number plates, Peter Sutcliffe was arrested in Sheffield. He was transferred to the custody of the West Yorkshire Police where he was questioned about the killings. Peter Sutcliffe confessed to the killings, stating that the voice of God had sent him on a mission to kill prostitutes.

"Good job too!" Al thought as he sat up on his bed.

The officer had a tray of lagers. He opened Al's cell door and handed Al four tins.

"That is something to celebrate, don't you think?"

"Absolutely," Al said as he ripped open the tin and began guzzling down the lager.

"What about me?" the black prisoner called out from the cell opposite.

"You have called me a hundred and one names and threatened to cut my throat countless times. Why would I want to share any of this with you?"

"Mate," Al called out. "If you promise to button it and treat the man with the same respect that he's shown here, then maybe, just maybe, he'd give you a drink too."

The police sergeant looked at Al and then back at the prisoner.

"I can do that."

"Good," the police sergeant.

"I'm Al, what's your name?"

"Tyrone."

The police sergeant opened Tyrone's cell door and handed over a tin of lager.

The three men shared the alcohol, agreed that Peter Sutcliffe should be hung, drawn and quartered for what he did to those innocent young women, and celebrated the arrival of another New Year. The police sergeant said that provided they kept a low profile he would allow booze and curries to be sent in, as well as conjugal visits. Al had to explain that a conjugal visit included sexual relations. Tyrone raised his tin and beamed.

The following morning Al was taken into the interview rooms where he was arrested for fraud. His finger prints had been found on the credit cards taken from Vodka Pat's apartment. He was also arrested for being fraudulently involved with over three hundred thousand pounds worth of social security books.

Black Sandra arrived later that same afternoon with one of her friends. As promised by the police sergeant, Al was given conjugal rights, but with both Black Sandra and her voluptuous friend, Janine.

Before she left, Black Sandra handed Al a large wad of cash that he was owed from Leaky. That evening Al paid for a bottle of whiskey and an Indian Curry to be sent in. Tyrone also had food and drink sent in from friends.

The mutually beneficial relationship worked well for all parties, until four small bags of heroin fell out of the food that Tyrone had had sent in. The police sergeant was severely pissed off and ready to shut down all privileges. Al managed to talk him round and had a few stern words with Tyrone, the junky. The privileges, including visits from Black Sandra and more of her friends, continued until Al developed a huge, extremely painful boil on his backside. He gritted his teeth and bore the pain, but no matter how much alcohol he consumed, the pain was relentless. Al was embarrassed, but eventually told the sergeant who, upon seeing it, had him shipped off immediately to HMP Brixton in an ambulance. The doctors examined the large pus-filled bump that Al had passed off as the consequence of a dodgy curry, and told him that he was lucky to be alive and should be dead.

The doctor explained that whilst some boils rarely cause further problems some, like his, develop inflammation and create open wounds. Al was told that had it not been treated it would have almost certainly poisoned his blood or developed an infection around the inner layer of his heart.

Chapter 14

Al, who was still on remand, was transferred to HMP Brixton in South West London. The Scottish prison officer known as 'Wee Rat' complained about his wages while walking Al through to his cell on C Wing.

"So get another job and stop bitching!" Al thought as he stepped into the single cell.

"It's a liberty," Wee Rat continued. "We can only have meat twice a week!"

"You're boring mate, and you stink of whiskey," Al thought as he nodded politely.

The following day Al was out on the wing when he recognised a friendly face.

"Leaky!" Al called out.

"Al!" Leaky called back before racing forward and shaking his hand enthusiastically.

"Fuck me you've put on some weight," Al said with a chuckle.

Leaky had become so fat that one roll of fat covered the next.

"Well it's all that good living," Leaky said.

"So what are doing in here? I would have thought you were far too smart to have got caught."

"Fitted up like a kipper."

"No way."

Leaky nodded.

"They told me to my face that they knew that I was printing forged fivers and was involved in giro's, cheque books, and passports, but because they had nothing concrete, they nicked me for... wait for it... living off immoral earnings."

"The bastards!"

"Tell me about. I've never taken a brass bean from a working girl."

"Yeah, but you've paid plenty," Al said with a chuckle.

"More than I care to remember," Leaky continued. "Blacks, Asians, redheads, blondes, brunettes. I've had them all in ones, twos and threes."

"You're not the only one," Al thought.

"What did you get?"

"I got three fucking years, Al. They had no evidence and zero statements, but still the copper got into the witness box and blatantly lied to the jury. I should have got off, I wasn't guilty, but on the word of one lying copper, the jury found me guilty and I got three years."

"It's wrong," Al said.

"I met one boke in here who got weighed off for twelve years for a robbery he didn't do and he's met a geezer in here who did it."

"The sad thing is mate, I'm not surprised."

"Oh, it gets better."

"Go on."

"The geezer who actually did the job was sentenced to a ten stretch for a blag he didn't do and was in Spain on holiday with his family when it happened."

"The Met is corrupt and rotten to the core," Al hissed. "They will take hand outs from one team of villains and stick the job on another set who don't play ball."

"Still, we'll do our bird and get out."

"Where are you working?"

"The laundry."

"Excellent, I've been given laundry too."

Leaky leaned forward and lowered his voice.

"I've got the delivery driver on the firm."

"Yeah?"

"Yeah, I have him bringing me in whiskey, in a plastic bottle of course, tobacco and Grecian 2000."

"Sweet," Al replied. "What's... Grecian 2000?"

"Yeah, well I have to keep this grey hair at bay. I've got my good looks to think about."

The two men chuckled as they walked towards the laundry. Al was assigned to a twenty thousand pound machine that required balancing. He was walked through the standard operating procedures. Al picked it up in minutes.

Later that morning the driver arrived with a van load of washing from HMP Holloway, a woman's prison in North London. Leaky did his bit of business and the driver left.

"Here, check this out," Leaky called out to Al as he unravelled a bed sheet.

As Al approached, a pair of knickers fell out onto the floor.

"What?" Al said as he looked down at the soiled knickers.

Leaky bent down, picked them up and held them up to his nose.

"Hmm," Leaky sighed as he inhaled deeply. "Sweet, sweet pussy."

"You're a sick man Leaky," Al said before roaring with laughter.

"It's good to have a real friend in here," Al thought as he watched Leaky unroll the sheets.

"Look at this."

Al read a message that had been written on the sheets:

'I need an eight inch cock deep inside me now!'

As Leaky sorted through the sheets they found other messages.

'Pussy is nice but cock is better'

'I dream every night about riding two hard cocks while Suzi licks my pussy'

'I'd love every con in the nick to cream pie my pussy'

"Bloody hell," Al thought as he read through the messages. *"These girls are worse than blokes!"*

"The girls must know that we get to read this stuff," Al said.

"Of course they do," Leaky said with a chuckle. "They probably get off on writing this stuff as much as we do reading it."

Leaky held up one sheet which had a prison number.

"Some of the lads in here send them letters."

"No way," Al said.

"Yeah and one mug actually married one of the girls who was sending this filth."

"He must have been off his head."

"Or just desperate."

The two friends read through all the explicit messages before placing the washing into the machines.

"It's good that you have the delivery driver on the firm," Al whispered.

"He's not the only one."

Al eyes lit up.

"I've got two bent screws bring me in whiskey too."

"Nice one!"

"I have to cough up twenty quid a bottle, which is a bit of a liberty, but there is no shortage of customers, so everyone is earning and getting what they want."

High up on the shelf was a portable Phillips radio playing *'Every Breath You Take'* by The Police.

"This is a sweet little number," Al thought as he watched Leaky re-reading some of the Holloway girl's messages. *"I've got a good, trusted, friend, access to whiskey, tobacco and other stuff, and there are two bent screws on the take."*

There was a third convict; a tall, muscular, black guy with long dreadlocks.

"What's his story?" Al asked.

"Noah Getachew," Leaky replied. "He ain't just got a chip on his shoulder, he's got the whole fucking bag!"

The two men watched Noah as he sat in front of the two chamber washing machine. His job was to ensure that the washing loads were equally balanced.

Just as *'Boxer Beat'* by JoBoxers came to an end, the Radio One presenter of the Breakfast Show, DJ Simon Bates, began to talk. The music to 'Our Tune' by Half Man Half Biscuit began to play.

"I like this," Leaky said as he dropped the laundry and looked up at the portable radio.

Simon Bates introduced 'Our Tune' every day. It featured a personal story submitted by one of the eleven million listeners, together with a song that had significance to the person or their situation. The stories included heartbreak, hope, sadness, grief, courage and friendship and were read out over Nino Rota's love theme from Franco Zeffirelli's Romeo and Juliet movie. The stories almost always ended with a tragic narrative which included illness or death.

Al stood by Leaky and listened to a heart breaking romance where the couple had a needless argument over a misunderstanding. The boyfriend, in a fit of rage, got on his motorbike and roared away. Simon Bates told the listeners how she was sorry for allowing the situation to escalate. The police arrived late at night and told her that her boyfriend had been in a fatal accident. The song that brought back the painful memories was *'Leader of the Pack'* by the Shangri-Las.

"They should include a few of the 'Dear John' stories that countless convicts receive in prison when the wives and girlfriends decide they need a new revenue stream to pay the bills, feed, clothe, and take them out." Al thought as the story ended. *"My mate hung himself after receiving one of them."*

A 'Dear John' letter is a letter sent in by the convict's wife or girlfriend. It generally starts with the ramblings of how they are, they miss their partner, but ultimately concludes with the message that they are moving on.

Leaky was quick to point out that not all the 'Our Tune' stories end in tragedy.

Later that day, as Al walked around the exercise yard he heard someone call out 'Jack, Jack!"

Al turned to see Davy Campbell, one of the lads he had been stealing lead with in Glasgow several years back. Al had never given his real name, and was known as Jack.

Al shook his hand warmly.

"I'd like to say that it's good to see you Davy, but it would have been better in a pub or somewhere outside."

Al explained that he was on remand and the outlook wasn't good. Davy Campbell told Al how he was doing four years for manslaughter. He had an argument with an Egyptian over money. Davy lost his temper and head butted the fella. Davy believed that he had just knocked him out, so he took the money which he believed was his, and left him unconscious on the floor. However the Egyptian had a heart attack and died.

Al thought how lucky he must have been to have battered men senseless over money, women and respect, but had walked away without any comeback.

The following day Leaky was strutting around the laundry with jet black hair as *'Is There Something I Should Know?'* by Duran Duran played on the portable Phillips radio.

"It looks like your Grecian 2000 has worked" Al thought as he chuckled to himself. *"I wonder if anyone has even noticed."*

The two friends sorted through the laundry and read the new messages that had been sent over from the girls in Holloway Prison. Leaky once again dropped everything he was doing to listen to 'Our Tune' read out by Simon Bates. As *'Love Will Keep Us Together'* by Captain & Tennille played, Al could hear the two-chamber washing machine rattling, shaking and thumping. Noah Getachew was sitting back in his chair just watching the machine operate out of balance.

"Here mate" Al said. "The machine isn't balanced."

"This is a twenty grand machine and working in here is a sweet number and I don't want you fucking it up for us," Al thought.

Al stood before Noah.

"Come on, do us all a favour and sort it out."

Noah looked up and snarled.

"You fucking rasclart!"

The term rasclart is a West Indian term which implies that the recipient is the blood from a woman's vagina after she has had her monthly period.

"Don't you fucking mug me off," Al said with a scowl.

Leaky bolted over and produced a six inch knife.

Al unclenched his fists.

"No, no, leave it out," Al said.

"I'll have him later," Al thought.

"I'll cut him a new arse hole," Leaky hissed.

"Just leave it," Al said with a sly wink.

Al and Leaky went back to reading some of the raunchy messages on the bed sheets.

Later that day Al watched as Noah Getachew was bigging himself up to a mate on the wing. Al could imagine that he was relaying some kind of fabricated story about how he put two tooled up rasclarts in their place.

Al watched Noah bump fists with his mate and then strut across the landing and go into the toilet. Al followed him in. Inside the toilet, Noah stood with his legs apart, urinating. Al bolted across the toilet and grabbed Noah by his long dreadlocks. He jerked him back and then swung him with all his might before releasing his grip. Noah landed on his side before rolling back and hitting his head against the wall. Al steamed forward and launched a powerful series of kicks in his body and head.

"Fucking mug me off!" Al called as he kicked and stamped on Noah. "Have this!"

Noah tried to protect himself by curling up into a ball. Al was having none of it. He reached down and grabbed his long dreadlocks until his face was exposed.

SMACK! SMACK! SMACK!

Al powered one vigorous punch after another into Noah's face. A single tooth broke and shot across the tiled floor.

"Leave it out man," Noah whimpered.

Al fired one last punch into his face before releasing his grip.

"Mug me off again and I'll fucking kill you!"

Al washed the blood off his hands before returning to the wing where the inmates were banged up until tea time. The incident had played over and over in his mind and he felt that there would be some kind of comeback, so he needed to inflict more violence. When the cell door opened, Al, without saying a word to anyone, walked at pace up to Noah's cell where he found him doing press ups with his top off.

"You'll need that and more!" Al said as he stepped into the cell.

Noah's face was heavily bruised and battered.

"I'm sorry man, I don't want any trouble."

Al was ready to steam forward and finish the job, but he could see that Noah was beaten, so he left the cell and went down for tea. Noah Getachew didn't come down for tea and stayed in his cell.

The next morning Noah approached Al on the landing.

"Are we cool?"

Al stepped back.

"Yeah, we're cool."

Later that afternoon Al spotted a familiar face on the wing. It was Jake McCullum.

When Al had first started operating around Kings Cross, Jake McCullum and his mate George McCoughlan were heavy duty villains and considered by many to be the up and coming force. They had a fearsome reputation for savage violence and had been slowly chipping away at Dougie 'The Man' McKinnon's Kings Cross Empire. An incident created by a working girl known as Nancy Fancy Pants, who had a thing for dangerous men, had placed Al on the front line facing them both. Al narrowly missed being stabbed by a bayonet, and punched, kicked and battered them both.

Jake McCullum looked over at Al and grimaced.

Al strode towards him.

"Have we got a problem?" Al said as he stood upright with his shoulders back and chest pushed out. "If we have, then we can sort it out here and now."

The stern look on Jake's face dropped into a smile.

"No, we don't have a problem."

Al stepped forward and held out his hand. Jake looked down at Al's hand and then back up at Al before shaking it.

In the laundry, Leaky had just taken delivery of two plastic bottles of whiskey and several pouches of tobacco. Noah was doing his job as the two chamber washing machine ran smoothly. While Leaky listened to Simon Bates tell another depressing story, Al sauntered over to Noah. He looked quickly from left to right before offering him a swig of whiskey from the plastic bottle.

Noah looked shocked. Al thrust the bottle forward.

"No strings?" Noah asked sheepishly.

"No strings."

Noah took the bottle and took a short swig. He closed his eyes and relished the taste.

"That was a free taster," Al said with a smile. "If you and your mates want some more, see me or Leaky."

"Yeah, cheers man."

"Al, Al McIntosh," Al said.

"Cheers Al."

Leaky was listening to Simon Bates intently. Once the story had concluded and *'When I need You'* by Leo Sayer started playing, the two men went back to reading the messages and loading the machines.

"The whole villainy game has changed," Leaky said.

"How do you mean?"

"This is the age of the Supergrass."

"Are you talking about Bertie Smalls?"

"Yeah, the slag."

Derek Creighton 'Bertie' Smalls was an old school East End career criminal. He led a team of armed robbers known as the Wembley Mob. They had pulled off an insider-led raid on Barclays Bank in Ilford, and got away with £237,736. It was considered a record at the time. The villains split up and headed for the Costa Del Sol where they sunbathed on the golden beaches while reading in the newspapers about how the Metropolitan Police were searching for them.

The mob stayed in Spain until the investigation lost its momentum and then one by one, they returned to the UK. Bertie Smalls was arrested in a suburb of Northampton and spent a Christmas in custody. His solicitor informed him that he would be looking at a minimum of twenty five years inside if convicted. Bertie Smalls called for a meeting with the lead inspector. He offered to name and incriminate his friends on the Barclays job and provide details of every criminal activity he had been involved with or knew of. With immunity from prosecution, Bertie Smalls became Britain's first Supergrass. Over fourteen months he provided the police with evidence that put twenty of his former criminal associates away for a total of three hundred and eight years.

"It was bad enough that he helped the police put his friends away, but he opened the doors for other slags to follow."

Career villains like Maurice O' Mahoney, one of Britain's most violent armed robbers in 1974, struck a similar deal and turned in one hundred and fifty names in exchange for a reduced sentence.

"All grasses will get what's coming to them."

At the end of giving his evidence at the Wembley Mob trial, the men sang *'We'll Meet Again, Don't Know Where, Don't Know When'* by Vera Lyn to Bertie Smalls.

"It comes to something when you do a job with someone and he's already collecting shit against you as insurance for if and when he gets caught."

"What's the answer?"

"Working with a small, tight, team or working alone."

"Or going straight."

***

Al was thrilled when he discovered that his friend, Jean Harlow, had been transferred to Wandsworth. It had been Jean Harlow and Mae West, two male prostitutes who worked Soho when Al first came to London, who had bought the starving young man fish and chips, found him a safe squat to stay and gave him work putting their business cards in telephone boxes. Al, Leaky and Davy brought Jean into the whiskey and tobacco distribution business. Combined, they had the sustainable supply routes to all markets and the muscle to protect it.

Black Sandra had visited Al and the two friends laughed about old times around Kings Cross and how disappointed they both were at not having a foursome with the two open minded punk rocker girls.

Wee Rat, the prison officer, was caught and prosecuted for credit card fraud, and Al learned that Leaky hid his knife between the rolls of fat on his stomach. Jean Harlow was doing eight years for half beating to death a punter who didn't open his safe quickly enough. It didn't take long for Jean Harlow to exchange blow jobs for drugs and tobacco. He became friendly with 'Pebbles', a male prostitute who looked and acted straight. Al had been supplying Pebbles with knickers that had been wrapped up in the prison laundry from Holloway. He had been caught wearing them on three occasions during a strip search, but he never named Al as the supplier.

Jimmy Watson was a prisoner on C wing that bred and tortured mice in his cell. He worked in the laundry on the machine next to Al's. Al had witnessed him snap their tiny legs before throwing them into a bucket of bleach in the laundry. Jimmy threw the mouse at the bucket and it bounced off, recovered and scampered away.

"You nasty bastard!" Al thought.

"Do you have to do that?"

Jimmy picked up a small white mouse and threw it into the bucket of bleach.

"They're vermin," Jimmy replied without looking up.

Al bounded over and grabbed him by the hair. He struggled as Al dragged him towards the bucket of bleach.

"If you ever do that again I'll fucking drown you in it," Al said as he pushed Jimmy's face over the bleach. "You're a fucking animal. I'm telling you now, your head will follow the next mouse that ends up in there!"

Al held Jimmy's face just a few inches from the bleach so that his message sank in before releasing his grip and leaving the cell.

"Sick in the head, people like that," Al thought as he walked back to his machine.

Later that day while crossing the landing, Al caught sight of an old enemy, John McQuaid.

"Fuck, this could get nasty," Al thought.

Al and his brother Brian were transferred to HMP Pentonville in 1977 before going on trial at the Old Bailey. On arrival they were pleased to find a pool table on the wing. When they started to rack up the balls another prisoner warned them that John McQuaid was the governor, number one on the wing, and no one got to play pool until John was up. Both Al and Brian ignored the warning and chalked their names up on the board. When John turned up there was an exchange of words while Brian had slipped off his shoe and was filling his sock with pool balls. John was due in court on the Monday, so he let it slide, but Al knew that their business was not complete.

Al spoke with a fellow inmate to get a message to John.

The following day the two men squared up on the landing with neither man backing off.

"We need to talk," Al said.

"So talk."

"Don't go playing the hard man with me," Al thought.

"Look we're both in here doing bird and if we go at it then we'll both get serious time, so let's let bygones be bygones."

"Is that it?"

"Yeah, that's it."

John McQuaid shrugged his shoulders.

"Agreed."

Al was happy that the two men had found a compromise and could co-exist on the wing without the need for violence and the potential of a heftier prison sentence.

The bathroom door locked firmly behind him, Al stepped into the bath and relaxed. He found himself thinking about all the men and women he had come into contact with since moving to London, and how many of them had been brutally murdered.

Al heard a scrambling noise. He looked up and saw John McQuaid had clambered up the dividing wall.

"What?" Al said as John dropped down into his bath water with a shank in his hand.

A shank is a handcrafted bladed weapon resembling a knife.

Al clambered awkwardly to his feet when John plunged the blade into Al's backside.

"Arghh!" Al yelled as the razor-sharp blade penetrated his skin.

Al threw a punch and lunged forward. They grappled ferociously with the blade cutting into Al's body. Al saw an opening and sunk his teeth into John's neck and bit down with all the strength he could muster. McQuaid cried out with his arms flapping around wildly and finally lost his balance. His legs buckled as he fell into the bath water. The two men were fighting ferociously for the right to live. Al managed to clamber on top of John while he thrashed around and began to punch the back of his head repeatedly before placing both hands on his head and holding him under water.

"Screws, screws!" Leaky hissed.

Al let go of John McQuaid's head. He rose from the bloody water, leant back and gasped for air. John's right eye was hanging out of its socket. Al scrambled out of the bath and opened the door. Leaky peered in, saw the shank, picked it up and placed it between the rolls of fat around his stomach.

Al had a stab wound in his backside and his nose had been pierced and broken by the blade. Leaky, while on bomb disposal duty, destroyed the shank.

Bomb disposal was the cleaning up of shite parcels that had been thrown from the cell windows during bang-up at night.

Chapter 15

Al was gutted when Leaky was transferred to HMP Blundeston, a category C prison in Suffolk and Davy went the following week to HMP Camp Hill on the outskirts of Newport on the Isle of Wight.

"You have visitors," the screw said to Al as he stood in the cell doorway.

"I'm not expecting anyone," Al thought as he rose up from the bed.

Al followed the prison officer through the wing and then to a room.

"Well it's not Black Sandra and one of her mates for certain," Al thought as he chuckled to himself. *"Now that would be nice."*

The prison officer opened the door and led Al into a room where two plain clothes police officers were sitting. Al looked at the screw, his solicitor and then at both the police officers before sitting down opposite them. The screw closed the door after leaving.

The two police officers introduced themselves before formally arresting Al for the murder of Jackie O'Docherty.

"Do you have anything to say?"

"It had fuck all to do with me," Al protested.

"What goes around comes around," the officer said with a wry smile.

"What is this, another fit up by the Mets boys in blue?"

"You're done, McIntosh," the second officer said as stood up. "Society will have a well- earned rest from you and your kind."

"How do you people sleep at night?"

"Extremely well, knowing that you're safely locked away."

The prison officer returned and escorted Al to the prisons D Wing.

The arrest for murder had catapulted Al to a category 'A' prisoner the highest in the UK. The category signified that the prisoner was high risk.

"This is fucking bullshit," Al thought as he was led onto D Wing. *"There are more crimes committed by the police and prison officers on criminals than we ever commit on society."*

Al had a sleepless night and he refused to leave his cell and go to work the following day. Having been briefed on events, the screws left him alone. A couple of cons knocked on his cell door and asked what was up. He shared the devastating news.

***

The following morning Al was processed and led to his new cell. His personal belongings were already on his bunk.

Al unpacked and lay on his bed with his hands behind his head.

"Murder; this is serious, and the bastards will be desperate to fit me up and make it stick," Al thought.

Al ventured out onto the wing where he was immediately stopped by a tall black guy with dreadlocks that ran half way down his back.

"You're new, right?"

"Yeah that's right.

"They call me scissor-man."

Al looked the prisoner up and down.

"Do you know why?"

"Is it because you're a fucking hairdresser?" Al thought

"I've killed two men with a bloody great pair of scissors, so they call me the scissor man."

Al watched as he walked back down the wing.

An hour later the scissor man reminded Al who he was and what he was in for and then again during the afternoon. Al got into a conversation with armed robber and Millwall fan John Hilton. The two men hit it off immediately. John explained that he was in for a wages snatch that was all going to plan until a 'have a go hero' thought he could take the team down single handedly. John shot him dead and was sentenced to hang, but was reprieved and given fifteen years. On his release he took up with old mates in Bermondsey and found himself out on the pavement robbing jewellers. The owner wouldn't play ball, so John put the double barrel sawn off shotgun in his face and then fired it into the ceiling. They got away with a good haul but were arrested a few weeks later. John was sentenced to another fourteen years inside.

From the corner of his eye Al could see Scissor Man approaching.

"Here, you!"

Al turned to face him.

"You know I've killed two men, don't you?"

"Yeah, because you've probably told me ten times today."

"Do you want to be the third?"

Al took two steps forward so his face was just inches from the scissor man.

"You need to clean your teeth you soapy bastard," Al thought.

"Scissor Man," Al said with his eyes burning into Scissor Man's. "I am the wrong person to be fucking with."

***

Al was working in a room sewing mail bags and found himself sitting next to a con he thought he recognised.

"Hello mate, I'm Billy, Billy Tobin," the prisoner said.

"Al McIntosh."

"You've probably heard of me," Billy said.

Al smiled.

"I think so."

Billy Tobin was the scourge of the Flying Squad and a prolific armed robber.

"Yeah I had plod all over London trying to take me and my boys down."

"What are you in for?"

Billy thrust his chest out and sat bolt upright.

"Armed robbery."

Armed robbers were considered prison royalty.

"Yeah I had those Metropolitan maggots following me all over London. I'd drive about in my gold Rolls Royce and give them a wave before disappearing into a club full of good looking birds."

"Why would you want to draw attention to yourself?" Al thought.

"A gold Rolls Royce?" Al said.

"Well, what's the point of making good money if you don't treat yourself?"

"I suppose so."

"You wouldn't see me in a gold Rolls Royce no matter how much cash I had sloshing about, let alone goading the old bill," Al thought.

"Yeah it was a fucking great life, booze, birds and being with your mates, and now I'm banged up in here"

"What did you expect?" Al thought. *"The old bill are corrupt and unless you're paying them off, this is where you end up."*

"I'll be forty by the time I finish this sentence," Billy said with a sigh. "What about you, what are you in for?"

"I'm innocent," Al said.

"Yeah, we all are in here."

Scissors, scissors, scissors," Billy called out.

The scissor man came bounding over to cut the thread on the mailbags. Al looked up and braced himself for violence. It didn't happen.

D Wing was filled with serious, dangerous, men where a single sign of weakness would almost certainly end in violence. Al liked Billy Tobin, he was funny and had a hundred and one stories to tell about his exploits. Al concluded that Billy just wanted to be seen and known. In the cell to his right was the man who murdered senior circuit Judge William Openshaw. John Smith had been sentenced to Borstal in 1968.He believed that the police and the courts were out to get him. John Smith decided that he would become Britain's most notorious assassin. He was seen, allegedly, waving his arms around and screaming obscenities outside the courts. The following day he stabbed Judge Openshaw to death at his Preston home which was right opposite Broughton Police Station. John Smith kidnapped a passing motorist and forced him to drive the six hours to Hawick in Scotland. Once arrested, John Smith was sentenced to life imprisonment for the high profile crime.

Al was told how the prison governor had sent two screws to bring John Smith to his office. However, John Smith understood all the prison rules and flatly refused, insisting that the governor should come to his cell, if he wanted to talk, and to make sure that he wiped his shoes before entering his cell.

Al struck up a conversation with John Smith and another con, Lee Hodges. They talked about life outside and their experiences inside. John Smith told them how he scaled Blackpool Tower to protest over prisoner's rights. The police had tried to talk him down, but he was adamant to stand up for something he believed in passionately.

"I was sitting on top of this tower looking down when I saw these kids playing in the sand. It brought back memories of me as a kid and the occasional trip to the seaside. One of the kids began to write something in the sand. I became quite excited, believing that I had some kind of support amongst the legions of angry old bill below," John Smith said with a sigh.

Lee Hodges was rolling a cigarette while Al listened intently.

"It broke my heart."

"What did?"

"That kid had written 'JUMP!' in huge letters."

"You're joking," Lee Hodges said, lighting the cigarette.

"I wish I was," John Smith said. "I just came down and gave myself up after that."

Al and John Smith became good friends.

The screws on D Wing moved the prisoners to different cells every two weeks. The rationale was that it didn't give them time to try and burrow their way out and escape. Al found the screws to be quite amenable as many of the criminals had very little to lose. When the cells were searched they would turn a blind eye to a little bit of weed. However if a prisoner played up then they were nicked. Category A was known as 'the book' because prisoners were photographed and their photo was put in a book and it went everywhere with that prisoner. It became handy when queuing for the doctors or dentist as screws would see the book and immediately took you to the front of the queue.

Category A prisoners were segregated from all other prisoners except at church on Sundays. Al was shocked but extremely happy to see Leaky back. He had been shipped back for fighting with another prisoner.

On May 26th 1982 one of the screws ran down the wing shouting:

'They've landed! The paras have landed on Goose Green and have engaged the Argentinians!"

Without exception every convict and prison officer roared 'Hoorah!' and punched the air.

In April 1982 the Argentinians invaded the Falkland Islands. A British task force was quickly assembled, including several airborne troop elements, to retake the islands.

"We might all be villains," Al thought as he punched the air for a second time while noticing that the screw had a military tattoo on his right arm, *"But we're all fiercely patriotic villains. We're proud of those paras and proud of our country."*

One of the cons started whistling the tune from the Bridge Over the River Kwai and everyone joined in.

Chapter 16

Al was being transported to the Old Bailey court for his trial.

The Old Bailey is the central criminal court for England and Wales where cases against people accused of serious crimes are tried by a judge and jury.

Al was handcuffed and locked away in a small cubicle on board a prison van. He found himself thinking about the arrival of the 'Awayday girls' from John O'Groats to Land's End and everywhere in between. Almost all of them had boyfriends or were married with children. The men in their life knew what they were doing and understood the reason why. The girls had no pimps leaching off their earnings. Kings Cross was a goldmine just waiting to mined. Al sighed when he remembered how he had been surrounded by beautiful girls laughing and joking in pubs where ninety nine percent of the customers were villains. Within a few months the girls had contacted their friends, sisters and cousins and told them how easy it was to make money in the pubs, illegal spielers, brothels and street corners. The prison van came to an abrupt halt and Al was taken down to the cells below the courts.

Al thought about the two girls who had taken it upon themselves to become 'union reps' for the working girls. They would collate information on dodgy, difficult and dangerous punters, create photo-fit pictures along with information about distinguishing marks, the make and model of their car and wherever possible the registration number. The girls would then place the information in and around all the pubs in Kings Cross.

"I could get life for Jackie Docherty's murder and I didn't even do it," Al thought as he sat on the edge of the prison bunk.

Al's thoughts wandered to Dublin Mary, the queen of the dippers, who would be expertly picking punter's pockets while the working girls were all over the men.

"That was my empire," Al thought as he looked up at the bars.

The prison officer lit up a cigarette outside his cell.

Al pondered over why a working class man would choose to become a police officer. His experience of both officers in Glasgow and London's Met were that they were all corrupt at some level. Officers in Glasgow had allowed Al and his crew to steal lead from the roofs of abandoned buildings, but for a price. Once the deal was done they would inform on their own kind if an arrest was imminent. In London he had experienced severe, savage, violence to try and get a confession for crimes he didn't commit, officers taking thousands of pounds in bribes to drop charges, and then make off to New York with the cash and charge the suspect anyway, and now he was being fitted up for a murder that they knew he hadn't committed.

Al thought about how and why the officers could create a plan, fabricate evidence, and lie in court in order to gain the conviction of a man they knew was innocent. The British police force being the greatest in the world, he concluded, was just extremely well manufactured propaganda for the politicians and the general public.

Al chuckled to himself when he visualised Leaky reveal a knife that had been concealed between the rolls of fat around his stomach.

His smile disappeared when he pictured the 'Note in the Box' on the wing where the grasses within the nick would grass up other prisoners.

"Scum," Al hissed.

Al thought about the bent screws who were selling plastic bottles of whiskey which were then watered down and sold on for tobacco, sweets and biscuits. He winced when he thought about how some of the screws would tell the known prison grasses that a convict they didn't like or had a run in with was a 'Peter Thief' and had stolen letters and pictures of another prisoner's wife.

A 'Peter Thief' was the lowest of the low. They would enter another prisoner's cell and steal anything that looked interesting, despite having little or no value. They were hated by both prisoners and screws. Al had witnessed a number of severe, brutal, beatings on innocent prisoners by misinformed inmates, who simply had a beef with a screw.

Al was led up the stairs by the bailiff into the court room, and placed alongside Bobby O'Neil who had also been charged with the murder, opposite the judge's raised wooden podium. Al briefly looked over at Bobby and then the jury before scanning the rest of the courtroom.

Al stood alongside everyone else in the court room when the judge entered.

The prosecution's barrister stood up and gave a brief summary of their case so that the jury could put it into context when the evidence was given. He concluded with: "We do not know why Mr

O'Docherty was killed but we think it had something to do with money."

"You think? You think?" Al thought as the prosecutor's words played over and over in his head.

The prosecution called their first witness. A young girl who looked as if she had been living rough on London's streets got into the witness box. Her speech was muffled when she finally took the oath.

"She's a junkie, a heroin addict," Al thought as he focused in on the dark circles around her eyes and pale complexion.

The girl slouched over the witness box and began to scratch and pick at the scabs on her face while the prosecution asked his questions. He waited patiently while the girl struggled with her words but finally said that she had heard a shot, looked out and saw the accused running down the stairs from the brothel.

"What?" Al thought. *"She's bloody lying. I'm being stitched up here!"*

The girl began to swoon as the prosecution asked her to repeat what she just said.

"I'm sorry but I really need the toilet," the girl said while steadying herself in the witness box.

The judge nodded and the bailiff took the girl through the courtroom.

"I never ran down the bloody stairs, I was running up them!" Al thought as he peered over at the two police officers whispering and then smiling.

A few moments later the bailiff returned to the courtroom and spoke to the judge and then to both the prosecution and defence. The judge adjourned the case.

Al's barrister informed him that the witness had gone to the toilets, injected herself with heroin and overdosed. The prosecution's witness had been rushed to hospital and Al was returned to HMP Wandsworth.

***

The court case resumed two weeks later with the young junkie back in the witness box. The prosecution asked their witness if she had taken heroin that day. She said no and was ready to complete giving her evidence. With a smug expression the barrister asked her to explain what she had witnessed.

"I heard what sounded like a gunshot, so I opened my front door to see what was going on and I saw that man running up the stairs."

Before the prosecution could, continue the judge spoke.

"This is very important madam. Can you please repeat the evidence you've just given?

The young junkie girl nodded.

"Yes, I thought I heard what sounded like a gunshot, so I opened my door and saw that man running up the stairs."

"YES!" Al thought as he tightened his right fist. *"I was running down Caledonian Road and up the stairs just like I said."*

The young junkie girl was taken from the stand and the second witness was sworn in.

"Big Jim Gibson!" Al thought as their witness gave his religion as being Scottish. *"I've always hated low life scum like you."*

Big Jim would not make eye contact with Al while he gave his evidence.

"Please tell me, in your own words, about your relationship with Mr McIntosh."

"Look at me you piece of shit," Al thought.

"Al can be found in most of the pubs around Kings Cross, They're all full of prostitutes and criminals. I'm not joking when I say that they're all thieves."

The judge immediately interrupted Big Jim and told the jury to ignore those comments. The prosecution continued.

"Al McIntosh offered me the contract to kill Jackie O'Docherty, but I turned it down."

"Please tell us what happened three days before the incident.

Big Jim took a deep breath and smiled.

"We were all in the pub having a few beers and chatting up the girls when Al has taken me into the toilets and showed me a 32-calibre pistol wrapped in a yellow duster."

"Those dirty, sneaky, bastards," Al thought. *"They've introduced this yellow duster to explain why there was no forensic evidence of or signs of gunpowder found in my pockets."*

"How did you know that the weapon was a 32-calibre pistol?"

"I am ex-military. I served in the army and so I'm extremely knowledgeable about handguns and rifles."

"You liar!" Al thought. *"Its lies, lies and more lies."*

"Please, tell the jury what happened two minutes after 11.00pm on the Caledonian Road on the night of the shooting."

"Yeah sure, I saw Al and his gang of cronies running up the Caledonian Road. He waved at me and called out 'How's it going'."

The prosecution's barrister sat down as Al's defence barrister stood up. He looked over at the jury and then at Big Jim Gibson.

"How well did you know my client?"

"I've known him for about two years."

"Do you like him?"

"No!"

"Why would that be?"

"He's been sniffing around my girlfriend."

"Are you sure that it was my client that was seeking the attention of your girlfriend or was it that your girlfriend had been seeking his attention?"

Big Jim became visibly agitated.

"I don't like him!"

The defence barrister looked at the jury, smiled, and then turned back to Big Jim.

"Would it be fair to say that he doesn't like you?"

Big Jim hunched his shoulders.

"My client doesn't like you."

"So what?"

"If my client doesn't like you then why would he take you into the toilets to show you a 32-calibre pistol wrapped in a yellow duster?"

Big Jim looked uncomfortable.

"Now remember that you do not like him and he most certainly doesn't like you."

"Well, he was probably just showing off and letting me know what a tough guy he was."

"Would it be fair to say that you dislike him because your girlfriend openly flirts around him?"

"He's a big head and a show off."

"Then why, I ask you again, would my client show you a 32-calibre pistol when my client has said openly to patrons of the pub that he doesn't like or trust you."

Big Jim shrugged his shoulders.

"My client believes that you are a police informer and he told you so, didn't he?"

"Yes."

"Then once again I'll ask you why my client, who believes that you're a police informer and shared his beliefs with other people in the pub, would take you into the toilets and show you a gun?"

"I don't know."

The barrister smirked and turned over the papers on his desk.

"On the night of the murder had you seen my client earlier?"

"No."

"So, you were walking down the Caledonian Road and you've seen my client running towards you, after the shooting, and then, knowing that you are a police informer he stopped and waved at you, knowing full well that you'll give evidence against him."

Big Jim was red in the face and clearly flustered

"What do you want from me?" Big Jim Gibson yelled out.

"The truth, we want to hear the truth."

The barrister looked at the jury and held out his open hand.

"We can all see that you're lying."

The barrister paused for a moment and the turned sharply towards Big Jim Gibson.

"Are you a police informer?"

Big Jim didn't answer.

"Do you know that police officer?" the barrister said, pointing towards the arresting officer.

"Yes."

"He is your mentor, isn't he?"

"Yes."

"Have you ever given evidence that secured a conviction?"

"Yes."

"Do you work for the police?"

"Yes."

"Are you a police informer?"

"Yes."

"So, my client was right about you all along. He didn't trust you and he told everyone not to trust you."

Big Jim was visibly perturbed and undid the top button of his shirt.

"My client never showed you any gun, did he?"

Big Jim remained silent.

"Please tell the court, have you been paid by the police to appear in court today and give this evidence?"

"No."

"Are you sure?" The barrister said as he picked up a file and held it up in his left hand.

"Yes... I was paid four thousand pounds."

"Have you ever been paid, by the police, to give evidence in a previous case?"

"No."

"What about in Manchester?"

Big Jim looked visibly distressed.

"Were you paid two thousand pounds for giving evidence in Manchester?"

Big Jim didn't reply.

"Mr James Gibson, you are an agent provocateur and you do this for a living don't you?"

An agent provocateur is a person who commits or entices another person to commit an illegal act or falsely accuses them of doing so.

"You are not a friend of my client, so why would he show you a gun and then, after the murder, stop while making an alleged getaway, and wave to you?"

Big Jim grabbed the bible and held it in his hand.

"I am not a liar! I am a man of God."

Al could see the prosecution barrister close his eyes and slowly shake his head.

The defence barrister asked the judge to have the trial thrown out.

The court room screw confided in Al and Bobby that during his thirty years of service this was the first time that two co-defendants had not tried to blame each other for the murder.

Al was taken to HMP Brixton.

***

A second murder trial date was set up but no witnesses turned up to give evidence. The judge directed the jury to return a 'Not Guilty' verdict and Al was discharged.

Two weeks later Al read in the newspapers that five of the six witnesses had been found dead. Big Jim Gibson had been escorted to a safe house in the Midlands and arrived at 1.00am. The police returned to take Big Jim back to the Old Bailey at 6.00am. However, Big Jim was missing. His personal effects were still on the premises.

Al was finally tried and found not guilty on a charge involving three hundred thousand pounds of stolen giros. He was also found not guilty of being involved in a sixty thousand pound fraud. Al McIntosh was finally convicted and sentenced to ten years for two counts of GBH and a single charge of fraud. He was transferred to HMP Parkhurst on the Isle of Wight as a category 'A' prisoner.

Parkhurst Prison, located on the Isle of Wight had a fearsome reputation. It was one of three high security prisons in the United Kingdom along with HMP Whitemoor and HMP Albany. HMP Parkhurst specifically housed some of the country's most dangerous criminals, earning itself a notorious status. It was known to have a strict regime and tough conditions designed to maintain control over the inmate population. The prison housed a mix of long term and high-profile prisoners, including those convicted of serious offenses including murder, armed robbery and organised crime. Many of the individuals were considered to be escape risks or had a history of violence. The prison's architecture and design were intended to enhance security. HMP Parkhurst had high walls topped with razor wire, surveillance cameras and a comprehensive system of gates and locks. The authorities' aim was to prevent any unauthorised access or escape attempts. The staff were believed to maintain a constant state of vigilance as they dealt with dangerous and volatile individuals on a daily bases.

Rumours of violence and clashes between inmates were not uncommon. Prisons were filled with stories about gang rivalries, power struggles and territorial disputes that often erupted into violent incidents. Among the UK inmates, the prison had become infamous for its riots and serious assaults, which sometimes resulted in severe injuries or fatalities. These incidents further added to the prison's reputation for being a dangerous and unpredictable environment.

While travelling down in the prison van Al found himself thinking about the men he had met in HMP Wandsworth and how their lives had led to them becoming category 'A' prisoners. He pictured Fast Eddie and Davy Campbell introducing him while walking around the prison yard:

"Here Eddie, tell Al about the thirty nine steps," Davy called out.

Al turned to see Davy winking at him.

"Nah, Al won't want to hear that."

"Yeah, I do," Al said.

"I don't know."

"I've got nothing but time," Al said. "Come on Eddie, tell me about the thirty nine steps."

Eddie took a deep breath and began.

"I was just fourteen when I was arrested and sentenced to hang."

"To hang, what for?"

"I killed two men."

"I'm not being funny, Eddie, but you have to be eighteen years of age to hang."

Fast Eddie shook his head.

"The judge made an exception in my case because the killings were so brutal."

Al motioned him to continue as they strolled around the prison yard.

"I tortured them to death."

"Why?"

"I wanted the number to their Swiss bank account."

"Did you get it?"

Fast Eddie shook his head.

"The silly bastards would rather die than give it to me."

"I'm shocked," Al thought. *"You can't spend fuck all on the other side."*

"The screws led me up the thirty nine steps," Fast Eddie said. "I counted each and every one of them and then I saw the noose. The hangman has placed the rope around my neck and this priest is rattling on about asking for forgiveness and to make my peace with God."

"Did you?"

"Did I fuck," Fast Eddie said with a chuckle. "I head butted the Lord's servant of the scaffold and watched him stagger around like a new born giraffe before collapsing to the ground. He was shaken but not broken."

"You're talking utter bollocks" Al thought. *"But I'll play along for fun."*

"Anyway, the hangman has pulled the lever and this other screw yells out 'STOP!'."

Al listened studiously.

"DON'T HANG HIM!"

"Bloody hell," Al said finally.

"HE'S BEEN REPRIEVED!'

Fast Eddie continued to tell Al how he was led back down the thirty nine steps with his neck still in place and alive.

"You were lucky."

"Yeah I suppose so," Fast Eddie said. "Did you know that I am the Kray Twins' favourite nephew?"

"I didn't know that."

"Yeah well its kind of common knowledge around here."

"Fast Eddie you are full of it," Al thought.

"I was the wheelman at the George Cornell murder. I was sitting outside the Blind Beggar waiting for Ron."

On the 9th March 1966, Ronnie Kray walked into the Blind Beggar pub in Whitechapel and calmly shot George Cornell in the head. He died in hospital several hours later. As children, the Kray Twins were good friends with George Cornell. He was a hard, fearless man who grew to become a prominent criminal in East London. When he moved to South London, he very quickly joined the Twins' major rival, the Richardson's, led by Charlie and Eddie Richardson.

"Ron walked out of the Blind Beggar bold as brass and just got into the motor."

Al put his hand into his trouser pockets and kicked a stone.

"On the way back to Uncle Ron's place I slapped his face red raw and told him that killing George Cornell like that was out of order."

"Delusional, I think he actually believes this shit himself," Al thought.

"Uncle Ron said that it was only because I was his favourite nephew that he stood for it."

The prison van drove onto the ferry that was destined for the Isle of Wight.

Al thought about a South London armed robber he had met on D wing.

"Nice guy, no ego," Al thought when pictured his friend, Joe 90 with his thick glasses. *"How the hell did he know where to point the gun with eyes like his?"*

Al chuckled himself.

Al remembered Joe 90 holding up one of the many mailbags to the screw peering down at the category A prisoners from his high chair.

"Are these mailbags really going to the post office?" Joe 90 called out.

"Don't ask me," the screw replied, shrugging his shoulders. "I only work here."

Al later discovered that the mailbags had no final destination and their only purpose was to give category A prisoners something to do. An image of Al strutting through the prison exercise yard came to mind.

"I shouldn't to be in here with all you bad boys," Al called out to Joe 90.

Joe 90 burst into fits of laughter.

"You, mate, are just as bad as the rest of us," Joe 90 said. "I've been reading about you in the newspapers.

Al knew that he was talking about the Jackie O'Docherty murder trial.

Al pictured himself and Davy Campbell sitting on the roof after stealing lead back in Glasgow.

Chapter 17

The prison van came to a halt by the gates of the notorious HMP Parkhurst.

"Well this is it, Britain's toughest jail and home to some of the country's most violent villains," Al thought as he peered through the window.

The gate opened and the van moved slowly forward into the jail.

"I'll need to keep my wits about me in here," Al thought as he peered up at the high walls topped with razor wire.

The van came to a complete stop and the doors were unlocked and opened.

"Here you are," the prison driver said.

Al looked at the building and then around to his left and then his right.

"Apparently no one has ever escaped this place," Al thought. *"I can see why."*

Al was met with a smile by the screw that led him through to the medical unit. He was polite and tried to engage Al in a conversation.

"If this screw is anything to go by, then the rest of them must be alright compared to the bastards at Wandsworth," Al thought.

Al was asked to sit outside the doctor's room. He looked up to see a prisoner leaning up against the wall.

"Hello mate," the Londoner said as he straightened himself up. "How long are you doing?"

Al looked the Londoner up and down and smiled.

"I'm doing ten." Al said as he sat up in the chair. "What about you?"

"I got life with a minimum of thirty years."

"Fuck me, that's serious time," Al thought.

"The screws here are alright compared to other nicks," the Londoner said. "They get to play football and don't work weekends."

"I'm Al," Al said as he stood up and shook the Londoner's hand.

"Reg. I'm on C wing."

"I'll see you about."

The doctor opened the door and ushered Al in.

The doctor didn't bother to look up at Al as he ticked the boxes on his forms.

"What is this, two arms, two legs and you're fit for work?" Al thought.

"You're fit for work," the doctor said without looking up.

"I may be fit for work but you are not fit for purpose," Al thought.

As Al was motioned to stand up, another inmate was ushered in.

"Here mate," the inmate said to Al. "Do you know that you were talking to Reg Kray?"

"Reg Kray!" Al thought as he sat back down on the chair outside the office.

"No way."

"Yeah, really."

"He doesn't look anything like the pictures in the newspapers."

"He looks old," Al thought.

"Straight up, that was Reg Kray."

Al thought about the stories he had heard about the Kray Twins and the images he had seen on the television and in the tabloids.

"Reg seemed like a nice fella, very pleasant," Al thought.

Al heard a high security door unlocking and a large screw stepped out. He was escorting a prisoner that Al recognised immediately.

"Peter Sutcliffe, the Yorkshire Ripper," Al thought.

Once the screw spotted Al, he stopped the Yorkshire Ripper.

"Oops, back, back," the screw said as he returned his infamous prisoner back behind the locked door.

"Fuck me, they're all in here," Al thought. *"That's Reggie Kray and the Ripper in one day."*

Al and his egg box full of books that he'd nicked from HMP Wandsworth were led down to the wings. B wing was on his right and C wing on his left. Al was led down to C wing where inmates were leaning over the rails and looking down. Al passed one inmate walking casually down the wing dressed in just a baggy pair of off-white underpants known as Y-Fronts.

"That's unusual," Al thought as the inmate disappeared into a cell.

Moments later Al was led into a single cell. He immediately spotted an envelope on his bed. On the front it simply read: Charlie Richardson.

Charlie Richardson was the leader of the Richardson gang which had been active in London during the 1960s. The gang had been involved in various criminal activities including extortion, armed robbery and violence. In 1966, Charlie Richardson and several members of his gang were arrested and put on trial. The trial was known as the 'torture trial' and gained significant media attention due to the brutal methods employed by the gang. It was alleged that the Richardson's used torture techniques such as electric shocks and nails through knee caps to extract money and information from their victims. Charlie Richardson was convicted in 1967 on multiple charges including GBH, assault, blackmail and fraud. He was sentenced to twenty five years in prison.

"I wonder if this was 'the Charlie Richardson's' cell," Al thought as he picked up the envelope and checked what was inside.

With the cell door closed, Al immediately dropped down and began his strict exercise regime. When Al had first been incarcerated he started doing a set of ten press up four times a day. He slowly increased it to twenty, then forty and was now completed one hundred press ups four times a day.

Exhausted, Al lay back on his bed with his hands behind his head.

"Well this is it," Al thought. *"This is your first day, so be a man, take no nonsense, and remember you've got no mates here, so you're on your own."*

Al allowed the memories of his time in HMP Wandsworth to visit as it became dark outside.

"Eddie the Trainers," Al thought as he chuckled out loud. *"What a character he was."*

Eddie the Trainers was a South Londoner and category A prisoner. He had been nicked for armed robbery and while being held at the police station, he requested a new pair of trainers as the ones he had been wearing at the time of his arrest had split. Reluctantly the police agreed and allowed his girlfriend to bring him down some new trainers. Eddie was led out to the reception area where he slipped the trainers on and then leapt straight over the counter and bolted out of the door and away into the back streets. He was, eventually, apprehended and sentenced. Al remembered how Eddie the Trainers had told him how he had been in hospital. The screws were supposed to stay outside the ward. When he discovered that they were slipping off he got dressed and left the hospital to carry out robberies and then returned to the hospital with the perfect alibi. Eddie the Trainers described himself as a luxury communist. Al liked him immediately.

Al looked up at the window.

"Ten fucking years!" Al thought before an image of a HMP Wandsworth inmate known as 'Down the Throat' entered his mind.

Down the Throat gained his vicious reputation as a lunatic because he would try and rip his victim's tonsils out. He thrived on violence and had seriously hurt numerous inmates for no reason. It had never been about money, like most prison conflicts, he had just got off on the violence. Al had heard that Down the Throat had a girlfriend he cared deeply about, but after being put away she soon found solace in the arms of a black guy from Stockwell. The new boyfriend had convinced her to go on the game and prostitute herself.

Down the Throat had always been a violent bastard but after hearing that his girlfriend had died from the Aids virus, the violence he inflicted reached new highs.

"I just can't understand people like that," Al thought. *"Making a pound note is the only thing that matters. Violence is always an option but should be a last resort."*

An image of armed robber Barry Reynard entered his mind:

"Al, I'm telling you some bastard from the pub grassed me up and got me fourteen fucking years."

"No mate, you grassed yourself up."

"What do you mean?"

"You've done the job, had it off with a few quid and then gone straight down the boozer, sunk half a dozen pints and told people your business."

"Yeah, but they were mates."

"So one bloke tells another who tells another and then every fucker knows," Al said. "You have to keep control of your tongue."

"Nah it ain't like that," Barry said. "Some worm grassed me."

Al chuckled to himself as he remembered the conversation.

"Barry just couldn't see that telling mates in the pub his business was his downfall," Al thought as he shifted around on his bed to get more comfortable. *"It's a shame because he was a nice fella."*

An image of a decapitated budgie falling to the floor popped into his head.

"That could have got nasty," Al thought.

There was an inmate on the wing that bred budgies, and as Al had entered his cell, he had inadvertently decapitated one of the budgies. It was a complete accident.

"What the fuck have you done?"

Al looked down at the decapitated dead budgie.

"Mate, I'm so sorry. I didn't see it perched on the door."

"That was my favourite budgie, Al."

"It was an accident."

"I've cared for that budgie since it was an egg."

"I feel terrible."

The category A inmate was serving life. His only interest was breeding budgies and selling them to other inmates.

The inmate looked down at the dead budgie and then back at Al.

"You breed budgies and sell them, right?"

"Yeah."

"Well why don't I give you two ounces of tobacco and you can think of this as you simply selling the budgie to me, okay?"

The inmate thought about Al's proposal for a few seconds and then smiled.

"Two ounces it is."

Al handed him the tobacco and left the cell.

"He was the kind of nutter that would fester on the death of his favourite budgie and just when you think it's all over and forgotten, he would stick a blade in your back," Al thought. *"It was money well spent not to be looking over your shoulder all the time. Besides, the only other option would be to do him, but that could cost me another ten years"*

Al could feel his eyes becoming heavy from the strenuous effects of a long day. He turned over and slowly fell into a deep sleep.

The following day Al ventured out onto the wing. Almost immediately he was approached by the inmate dressed in just his underpants.

"Alright mate," the inmate said in a thick Glaswegian accent.

"Yeah, good," Al replied.

"Do you play football?"

"No, not my game."

"Oi, you, fuck off!"

Al turned to see a guy approaching.

"Is this about to go off already?" Al thought as he clenched his fists.

The Glaswegian took one look at the guy approaching and shot off across the wing.

"I've just heard your surname down the wing."

"Yeah, what of it?" Al said.

"Do you have a brother?"

"Yeah."

"Is his name Brian?"

"Yeah, it is," Al replied with a look of surprise.

"We were good pals, I'm Mackie," the inmate said, holding out his hand.

Al shook it.

The two men talked at length. Al discovered that Mackie had been a jockey in his teens and was destined for big things with a series of fifth places. Then suddenly he had an unexpected growth spurt and shot up to over six foot tall. All his dreams of being a professional jockey and joining the horse racing circuit evaporated.

Later that night, Mackie brought some prison made hooch, a bong and some cannabis into Al's cell. Al had never smoked cigarettes and so smoked the weed direct from the bong while Mackie rolled up joints and sipped on his cup of hooch.

Hooch is prison slang for alcohol made within the prison walls.

"Mackie seems like a nice enough fella," Al thought just before the cell door was flung open.

"Mackie, you two bob slag. Where's my fucking drug money!"

Al later learned that the inmate chasing an outstanding drug debt was South London Armed Robber, Joe Moody.

Mackie was up and kicked the cell door shut in seconds. He grabbed a chunk of wood and began to batter Joe Moody around the head.

"Who the fuck do you think you're talking to?" Mackie yelled out as he battered Joe around the head over and over.

Joe threw several sloppy punches but Mackie was all over him with kicks, punches and strikes to his head with the lump of wood. Al watched as Joe's legs began to buckle. Mackie grabbed him by the scruff of his neck, opened the cell door, and threw Joe Moody out onto the wing.

"You walk in here, uninvited, and try mugging me off in front of my pal?" Mackie hissed. "Go on, fuck off!"

"Oh fucking great, Al thought. *"My first night here and I'm guilty by association."*

Mackie returned to Al's cell and shook his hands and fingers.

"You can't be putting up with shit like that," Mackie said. "I'm not scared of him or the South London mob."

"Oh great, so now it's a mob," Al thought as he listened to Mackie.

"You can't afford to show any weakness in here," Mackie continued. "I'm not scared of anyone and I'll tell them!"

"Do you owe him?"

"Yeah, but that's not the point, Al," Mackie said vehemently. "If I let Joe Moody talk to me like that then it'll open the flood gates for others and I'll be fighting wannabe mugs seven days a week. So no, fuck him, approach me with respect and he'll get what's owed.

"You're a nice fella, Mackie, but with an attitude like that you could cause trouble in an empty house," Al thought. *"Still, any friend of Brian's is a friend of mine."*

***

Al was given a job in the laundry alongside bank robber Johnny Dee and Bermondsey Kevin. Al's job was to place washed shirts on a mannequin and then steam would belch out and all the creases were gone. It was Kevin's job to fold the shirts.

Al felt a twinge in his stomach, so he disappeared off to the toilets. As Al pulled the chain he heard somebody outside. Al opened the door cautiously. It was Bermondsey Kevin.

"Fancy a line?"

Bermondsey Kevin held up a huge bag of powder.

"Look at the fucking size of that bag," Al thought.

"That's just party time stuff to me," Al said.

"So have a line and imagine you're at a party," Bermondsey Kevin said. "It's got to beat ironing and folding shirts, right?"

"He must have a screw on the payroll to have a bag like that," Al thought.

"What do you want for a line?"

"Nothing."

"Nothing? No catches?"

Bermondsey Kevin shrugged his shoulders and laid out a line of the fine white crystal powder for Al.

Al bent down and held his finger over his right nostril and then sniffed the party powder deep into his nasal passage. As Al stood up he felt an immediate euphoric sensation. He felt excited, energetic, confident and sociable. Al and Bermondsey Kevin chatted, laughed and told funny stories while their brains experienced a temporary jolt of stimulation from increased dopamine production.

"That's good gear," Al thought as he enjoyed its euphoric effects. *"There's not too much corn flour, talcum powder or flour mixed in this."*

The high lasted a little over fifteen minutes.

"That came on hard and fast," Al thought as they re-joined the lads in the laundry.

Once work had finished, Bermondsey Kevin strutted across the wing to his South London mates and Al joined Mackie and few other lads.

"What's your take on Brinks Mat, Al?"

The Brinks Mat robbery took place on the 26th November 1983 at the Heathrow International Trading Estate and was one of the largest robberies in British history. Twenty six million in gold bullion, diamonds and cash was stolen by a South London firm of six men led by Mickey McAvoy and Brian Robinson. They were both arrested just ten days after the robbery.

"I don't think about it that much," Al said as he shrugged his shoulders.

"They're proper villains, Mickey and Brian."

"Yeah, nice fellas."

"I heard it was over three tons of gold, imagine that."

"Three tons? That's got to be, what, six or seven thousand bars?"

"That's dream time stuff."

"Fancy using your brother in-law."

"Tony Black grassed on them."

"That was the lead, though. I mean, it's all risk and reward."

"That gold will be up for grabs now."

"Not a chance, Mickey will have good, trusted, mates with his share."

"Not from inside."

"He's not the kind of fella to mess with."

"There will be murders."

Al listened to the Brinks Mat Robbery debate. It was to become a regular topic of conversation throughout his time in prison. He thought about the Brinks Mat job and if it had been carried out by him, Brian, Leaky and couple more of the active villains around the Kings Cross area.

"I'd like to think that I could trust my brother and the Combination, but twenty-six million pounds buys a whole lot of freedom and they're all villains."

Chapter 18

It didn't take long for Al to discover that HMP Parkhurst's C Wing was almost like a psychiatric ward with seriously disturbed men thrown in with hardened criminals. Al had estimated that one in three of the men on his wing were nut jobs and were kept heavily medicated by Dr Cooper to subdue and control their behaviour. The medication didn't always arrive at the times when it should have, resulting in violent outbursts. One prisoner that Al had befriended, Peter, was medicated daily. When the drugs didn't arrive, he would smash up everything in his cell. Peter, despite being very capable, would never vent his frustration and anger on other cons or screws. Al had witnessed this many times and thought it was sad to witness Peter become so distressed. Al liked him.

Al heard that Fast Eddie from Wandsworth had been released and on the outside he decided to rob a bank. Al knew that in reality Fast Eddie was a petty thief who specialised in stealing personal protective wear from hospitals, but he liked him and considered Fast Eddie to be harmless. The story was that Fast Eddie acquired a replica hand gun and stormed into a bank waving it around and demanded that the cashiers fill bags with cash. They did as they were ordered and Fast Eddie had it on his toes. However, he hadn't thought through his escape plan. Once outside, while carrying the gun in his right hand and a bag of cash in his left, he thrust the replica firearm into the face of a waiting taxi driver and ordered him to drive. The taxi driver rammed the shifter into first gear and screeched away. As he raced through the gears, Fast Eddie was being thrown around on the back seat. The taxi driver took a sharp right hand turn to cross a bridge over a canal. With Eddy still struggling to sit upright and hold onto the cash, the driver came to a screeching halt. The driver clambered out of the driver's side door and raced around to the back door. He tore the door open and proceeded to batter Fast Eddie's face with a rapid succession of punches before climbing on his chest and pinning his shoulders down. Fast Eddie was held until the police arrived and hauled him away.

Out on the exercise yard Al caught up with him.

"It's good to see you Eddie," Al said. "Just a shame that it's in here."

"Tell me about it," Eddie said. "I had it all planned out. A nice little tickle at the bank and then off to Spain to live in the sunshine, shag birds and hang out with proper people.

Al chuckled to himself.

"Well since you're here, Eddie, are you going to introduce me to your uncle Reg?"

"I can't Al, Uncle Reg told me to keep it quiet."

"What, about you being his nephew?"

"Yeah."

"Why would he do that?"

"I don't ask questions, Al. If Uncle Reg said to keep my mouth shut then that's what I'm going to do."

"I just want a quick introduction, you know, hi Uncle Reg this is my friend Al McIntosh."

Fast Eddie was visibly perturbed.

"Eddie."

"What?"

"You're not a nephew to the Twins, are you?"

Fast Eddie began rubbing his hands together. He was clearly distressed.

"No, I'm not, but please don't tell Reg. I don't want to get bumped off," Eddie whispered.

Al was later told by another inmate how Fast Eddie actually got his nickname. He had been christened with it while serving time in Borstal as he was the slowest man in the place on film night and all the other prisoners had to wait until he turned up.

"Your secret's safe with me," Al said with a chuckle.

Another inmate by the name of Leicester Lee, joined them.

"Alright?"

"Yeah, you?" Al said.

Fast Eddie remained quiet and walked on with his head down.

"You were mates with Joe 90, in Wandsworth, right?"

Al instantly thought about his South London friend with his thick glasses and smiled.

"Yeah, he's a good friend of mine," Al said as he turned to face Leicester Lee from a few cells down. "We met in Wandsworth, why?"

"I heard that they transferred him to Maidstone nick in Kent and he tried to escape."

"Can't say I blame him as he was serving fourteen years the last time I saw him," Al thought.

"The official story is that some fat bastard of a screw wrestled him down and sat on his chest and crushed him."

"Do you mean...?"

"Yeah, sorry mate, but he's brown bread."

Al understood brown bread to be slang for dead.

"The unofficial story is that he was so badly beaten that they put the story out about the salad dodging screw as a cover up story."

"Bloody hell, I really liked Joe 90," Al thought as he visualised him waving across the prison exercise yard wearing his thick glasses.

"I heard that his old lady was queuing in the waiting room to visit him."

Al closed his eyes and slowly shook his head.

"I hope that all this is just old wives tales and my pal, Joe 90, is alive and well," Al thought.

"I hope it's all bollocks," Al said.

"It came from a good source."

"What a damn shame!" Al thought as he visualised his wife being told the devastating news.

The two inmates walked in silence for several seconds.

"I'm sorry to be the bearer of bad news."

"It ain't your fault."

"I was sure that you were mates, so I thought it only right that you should know."

"I appreciate it, thanks."

Leicester Lee inhaled deeply.

"Frankie Fraser was in Wandsworth about the same time as you," Leicester Lee said. "Did you meet him?"

Al shook his head.

"I saw him for about two minutes and that was it."

"What was he doing?"

"He walked over the centre spot, which is forbidden, stopped and did a little shoe shuffle type dance to piss off the screws."

"That sort of thing has cost him a lot of prison time," Leicester Lee said.

"It didn't impress me," Al though as he pictured Mad Frankie Fraser doing his dance.

"He's done way more bird than he should have."

Mad Frankie Fraser was kept separate from the rest of the category 'A' men.

"The only time was when he shouted out from his cell to everyone refusing to come in from the exercise yard."

"What was it, some kind of protest?"

"We made out that we were protesting about the food but the truth was that it was a Saturday night and we knew that the screws pissed off home early."

"Nice one," Leicester Lee said with a chortle.

"Yeah, they had to stay and try to coax us all in. At first they started dishing out direct orders to cease the disobedience."

"I bet that didn't go down well."

"We told them to shove their orders up their arses."

"Yeah."

"Yeah, they then climbed down off their big inflated egos and tried to bribe us with a decent fry up."

"Do love a fry up."

"The only con to break ranks was Billy Tobin."

"What, you mean Billy Tobin the bank robber?"

Al nodded.

"He went down in a lot of people's estimation that day."

"I can't believe that he could be so traitorous."

"Me either."

"What was Frankie Fraser saying?"

"He was just hurling abuse at the screws, mate, you would not believe the language, but he was backing us all up."

Al pictured armed robber Joe 90.

"Joe 90 was fuming when Billy fucked off and left us."

"I often think of you mate," Al thought. *"I hope you're still with us."*

***

Al was in Reg Kray's cell drinking hooch and chatting with Freddie Sewell aka Fat Fred.

"I think of the screws as my servants," Reg said with a grin. "They open my door for me in the morning and close it again at night."

The three men chuckled.

"Fuck me, Reg Kray and fat Fred have both got Chesterfield chairs in their cells, how do I get one?" Al thought as he sipped the prison made hooch.

Al had heard the stories about Fat Fred and his team.

The press had dubbed Fat Fred and his team of four lads the Crazy Gang after pulling off a jewellery heist. He had been told how they were all proper tooled up and armed to the teeth with shotguns, handguns, the whole nine yards. Fat Fred had a place in Blackpool and had seen the jewellers and all the gear they had on show. It was to be a big job with gold, jewellery, and watches. Al was told how Fred and the lads had driven up to Blackpool and plotted up in a guest house. They were convinced that it would be a doddle and a nice little earner. Tim, the con telling the story, told him how they kicked the door in and started waving the shooters about. The Londoners were all over the jewellery in seconds and piling it all into bags. The staff had shit themselves and gave no resistance."

240

Tim reckoned Fat Fred and his mob had about two hundred grand's worth of gear. One of the staff had pressed a silent alarm button that went straight to the old bill station and the next thing they knew was the sound of sirens wailing and they knew it was about to come on top.

Al remembered listening intently to Tim telling the story.

"The Londoners had it on their toes and bolted out to the getaway motor when some have-a go-hero has tried to stop me, so Fat Fred clumped him good and proper. They've started the motor and roared off down the street with the old bill hot on their tail. The bastards were closing in, so the driver came to a screeching halt and they clambered out when a copper has run towards them. He was shot in the chest and then they hijacked a butcher's van at gunpoint. It came on top so they ran off in different directions. Fat Fred had two old bill chasing him down an alleyway which turned out to be a dead end.

Fat Fred shot one of them and he went down and then this other copper has tried to wrestle his gun off him. Fat Fred shot him twice in the stomach."

Al had imagined Fat Fred annoyingly rubbing his hands together and saying that it was the worst day of his life.

PC Carl Walker was shot in the groin and Chief Superintendent Gerry Richardson was shot dead. The manhunt for Fat Fred in 1971 was the biggest of its kind with wall to wall television and press coverage. The police put up an astonishing ten thousand pounds reward. Fat Fred was caught forty five days later while relaxing on a sofa in an Islington bedsit. He was found to have a loaded shotgun by his side. All five robbers were convicted for a combined total of ninety three years.

As Reg and Fat Fred spoke, Al thought about the countless stories he'd been told about the police fabricating evidence and lying outright under oath in a court of law to secure a conviction.

"The old bill are lying, low life, bastards," Al thought. *"They claim to be defenders of justice and yet they break more laws by fitting up more suspected criminals than crimes the criminals have inflicted on society."*

***

Later that afternoon Al stopped by his friend's cell only to find that he had been ghosted to another prison.

"Sorry pal."

Al looked down to find a Palestinian on his prayer mat.

"I was looking for my mate."

Al noticed a poster of the Ayatollah Ruhollah Khomeini, the Iranian political and religious leader, who was serving as the first supreme leader of Iran.

The inmate introduced himself as Hassan and Al engaged him in conversation. Hassan had made a carrot curry and invited Al to share the meal with him. Al agreed and chatted with Hassan for a couple of hours:

Hussain Ghassan Said was one of three men who approached Shlomo Argov, the Israeli Ambassador, as he got into his car outside the Dorchester Hotel in Park Lane. Armed with a WZ63 machine gun, he shot Shlomo Argov in the head. Argov was not killed but critically injured and after the terrorists made their escape, he was rushed to the National Hospital for Neurology and Neurosurgery. Hussain and the Palestinian splinter group were arrested in a London flat and sentenced to thirty to thirty five years.

Hussain told Al that he had no fear and believed passionately in paradise after death.

"That would make you one very dangerous man," Al thought.

Al was the only inmate who spoke with Hussain.

Later that day Al learnt that his friend Davy was dead. He sat on his bed and visualised himself and Davy sitting on the roof of a house, having just stolen all the lead.

"My friend, Davy One Leg, the man who got away with murder," Al thought.

Davy One Leg was a pools winner who lived in a flat around Kings Cross. No one knew exactly how much he had won, but theories started from as low as ten thousand pounds to several hundred thousand pounds. Davy enjoyed a good drink and on special occasions, drugs. Two local villains, Jake and Johnny Boy, decided to befriend Davy and try to get their hands on his money. They plied him with drink before leaping over and ripping off his wooden leg and beating him with it. When he refused to give up his money they dragged him out to the balcony and hung him, by his leg, from the fourth story. Finally they pulled him back to safety. The two villains decided that they would take a second go at prizing cash out of Davy. However this time Davy was ready and he spiked both their drinks with a powerful sedative. Jake and Johnny boy collapsed.

Davy, driven on by the powerful memory of hanging from his four story balcony, beat them both with a hammer while they lay unconscious. The two men died from their horrendous injuries and Davy was arrested and charged with murder. Davy had convinced the jury that he feared for his life and a slew of witnesses came forward saying that they saw what Jake and Johnny Boy had done to Davy.

Chapter 19

"*93, 94, 95, 96, 97 ,98, 99...100,*" Al counted in his head before leaping up onto his feet.

Al had just completed the third set of one hundred push ups that day. He felt a deep sense of satisfaction and accomplishment after pushing his body to its limits. The tough exercise regime released endorphins, a natural mood-boosting chemical in the brain. Al threw his head back and inhaled deeply as the sense of euphoria washed over his body. He clenched and unclenched his fists several times as the enhanced mental clarity and focus kicked in. Al shook his hands and arms. His mind was sharper and more focused, and he was ready to tackle tasks with more efficiency and effectiveness.

"Right, let's do it!" Al thought as he left his cell and strutted down to the shower block.

He approached the shower block with caution, looked in and saw his target washing his face in the sink. With absolute clarity Al raced over and grabbed his target by the head. He battered it into the sink three times before lifting up him with the soapy water dripping down his face.

"What the...?"

SMACK...SMACK ...SMACK!

Al delivered a rapid set of left and right hooks before his target slumped against the wall.

"You bastard!" Al yelled out as he kneed his victim in the groin.

"Urghh!"

SMACK...SMACK...SMACK!

Al drove his fist hard into his victim's stomach twice, before stepping back and delivering an almighty right hander that sent his target crumbling to the tiled floor.

"Don't you ever fucking talk to me!" Al hissed before kicking the victim hard between his legs

"You make me sick to my stomach!" Al said before sticking the boot in three more times. "Try talking to me again and I'll fucking kill you!"

With his victim lying flat out on the floor with blood running down his face, Al turned swiftly on his heels and bolted out of the shower rooms and made his way back to the wing.

The day before, Al had been chatting innocently to a guy in the shower rooms. He had seemed like a nice enough fella until he returned to the wing and discovered that the guy had killed all three of his children. Mackie told him that his defence was 'I gave them life so I have the right to take it.'

Al had decided there and then to deliver the kind of prison justice that all nonces, sex offenders and people who harm women and children deserve.

Nonces, sex offenders and inmates who commit crimes against woman and children are hated by inmates with a passion. Given the opportunity, it was considered an inmate's duty to attack them. Many of the inmates have children or siblings on the outside and they immediately associate the act with those they love and care about. The prison populations may have been thieves, armed robbers, murderers or committed violent crimes, but their moral compass is crystal clear when it comes to sex offenders. The only good nonce is a dead nonce.

High profile sex offenders are kept locked in their cells.

"Are you alright, Al?" Mackie asked as he approached him and group of lads.

"Yeah, I just needed to take care of a bit of business."

"Is it sorted?"

"Oh yeah," Al said.

"Sweet," one of the South London lads said.

When the lads began to speculate about the Brinks Mat gold, Al chose to stroll down to the television room. Reg Kray and a few of his close friends were in the little cooking room. He was cooking a pan full of sausages.

"My brother and I will be released one day," Reg Kray said.

"Of course you will."

"Do you have any plans?"

"Yeah, Ron and I will get a little place down in the country."

"That'll be nice."

"Yeah and I'm going to marry Maureen."

Maureen Flanagan was Violet Kray's hairdresser and a close friend of the family. She was an actress and a popular tabloid model with regular page 3 features in The Sun newspaper. In her twenties, Maureen was the most photographed model in Britain. Her career grew to encompass television appearances and roles in The Benny Hill Show, Monty Python's Flying Circus, The Dave Allen Show, The Likely Lads and Only Fools & Horses.

"She's gorgeous!"

"Stunning!"

"I had a pic of her in my cell, she's lovely Reg."

"Her legs were insured for twenty five grand, cracking pair of pins."

"Wasn't she in that Dracula 72 movie?"

"Yeah, she played alongside Christopher Lee."

"Didn't she also play the lead in a Danish movie?"

"Yeah, it was 'The Love Lives of Cynthia' ."

"Wasn't that Cynthia's Sister?"

"Same movie."

"Maureen wrote a book too."

"Did she?"

"Yeah, my old woman bought it."

"What was it called?"

"The Intimate Secrets of an Escort Girl."

"She's quite the talent, Reg, I'm sure you'll make a great couple."

"Yeah, just as soon as Ron and I are out."

Al remembered seeing pictures of Maureen on prison cell walls in every prison he'd been locked up in.

"I hope it all comes off the way you want Reg," Al thought before leaving the London lads with their sausages.

"Alright, Tommy," Al said as his friend passed him on the landing."

"Yeah, good Al.

"Where did you get the new sweater?"

"Nottingham got it for me."

Al shook his head.

"For fuck's sake Tommy, I told you about him."

"Nah, he's alright

"I'm telling you Tommy, he's grooming you; the bloke is a homosexual predator."

"Nah, trust me Al, he's alright."

"Think about it, one minute he's buying you stuff, then he asks if he can suck your dick and then who knows?"

"That's not him."

"Alright Tommy, it's on you mate, but you were warned."

"Yeah, yeah, catch you later."

Nottingham had been refused entry to a nightclub by the bouncers. He was bitter, angry and wanted retribution. He strolled up to a petrol station, bought a can and filled it with petrol. Nottingham returned to the club, doused the place in petrol and then locked the doors right after setting fire to the place.

Al was chatting with Mackie on the landing when suddenly Tommy came running out of Nottingham's cell screaming his head off and repeatedly smashing a coffee mug into his face.

"I knew it," Al thought. *"He's fucking done you just like I said he would. Why aren't you smashing him in the face with the coffee mug?"*

Tommy ran up the wing screaming at the top of his voice with blood streaming down his face

Nottingham had closed the cell door, held a knife to Tommy's throat and threatened to take his life. He aggressively removed Tommy's trousers and underwear before pinning him down on the bed and raping him.

"Nottingham's a nasty piece of work," Al thought. *"One of these days he'll pay the price for messing with straight lads."*

"I saw that coming," Captain Birdseye said to Al as he passed him.

Captain Birdseye had been given the name because he looked just like the actor who played the part in the television advert. Mackie told Al that Captain Birdseye had murdered his nagging wife and stuffed her dead body in a freezer along with the fish fingers. She'd been stored away for almost two years. With summer arriving, Captain Birdseye booked himself a package holiday to Spain for a couple of weeks. However, while he was away, there had been an electrical power cut and the freezer had defrosted. On his return from the Costa Brava Captain Birdseye was arrested and convicted.

Chapter 20

"**I** fucking hate the English!"

"But why Brackie?"

"They're arrogant."

"Surely not all of them?"

"Fuck the lot of them and the Irish."

"What, you hate the Irish as well?"

"But why?"

"They keep banging on about the fucking world cup!"

"Brackie, that was 1966."

"Yeah and they're still going on about it!"

"Really?"

"Yeah and that bastard Cromwell."

"Oliver Cromwell?"

"Yeah, those English marching up to Scotland… raping and pillaging."

"Yeah, but not recently."

"I don't give a toss, Al, I hate them all and I'll never change my mind."

"So why did you come down to England?"

"For work."

"What, was there no work in Scotland?"

"Yeah but the pay is better in England."

"So you're happy to come down to England to earn good money but you still hate the English."

"You've got it in one."

Al was chatting with Brackie the Scot and Patsy John.

"Patsy."

Al, Patsy and Brackie turned to see a familiar South London figure.

"Yes mate."

"You owe us for gear."

"Yeah, I'm skint, you'll have to bear with me."

"You ain't skint Patsy, we know you've been buying gear from B wing."

"I told you I'm skint, but you know I'm good for it."

"We're sensible people, Patsy, but six weeks is now taking liberties."

"I'll get it sorted, alright!"

"We don't want to be chasing you for money again, Patsy."

The South Londoner turned and returned to the group of men.

"For fuck's sake, we're talking about ten quid!"

"It's not the money with those lads," Al said.

"I'll fucking show them," Patsy hissed before storming off.

Ten minutes later Patsy passed Al and Brackie carrying scores of Mars bars in his arms.

"This won't end well," Al thought as he watched Patsy kick a cell door open and disappear into one of the South London lad's cells.

Patsy had bought ten pounds worth of Mars bars, stormed into a cell where several heavy weight villains, including Reg Kray, were engaged in conversation. He looked around before throwing the Mars bars up in the air and yelling "There's your fucking payment!" before marching out and returning to Al and Brackie.

Al shook his head.

"You shouldn't have done that Patsy."

"Fuck them, I'm no fucking mug!"

"Neither are they," Al thought.

"They're not going to stand for that," Al said.

"I don't give a toss, Al," Patsy hissed. "I'm not going to let anyone, anywhere, mug me off."

Later that afternoon while Patsy was walking around the exercise yard, a South London con came up behind him and thrust a prison made shank. He narrowly missed Patsy's back as Patsy had turned around. The shank went straight through Patsy's hand and cut deep into his thumb.

Although the South London lads were not the easiest to get on with, Al had built friendships with most of the lads. As a rule, Londoners, Blacks, Scots and Irish generally stick to their own.

***

The following morning Al was chatting in his cell with Mackie when he heard a knock on the door.

"Yeah, come in," Al called out.

"Alright lads," Reg Kray said as he entered Al's cell.

"Yeah, you?" Al said with a hint of surprise by the visit.

"We had a right night and there's nothing left for a hair of the dog," Reg Kray said. "The screw who normally flogs us booze is away on holiday."

Al and Mackie listened as Reg went on to say that his wing was dry.

"I don't have anything," Al said, shrugging his shoulders.

"I've got a quarter ounce of cannabis," Reg said with a grin.

"Reg, I've got stuff brewing, but its only three days old. It won't be good."

"I'll have it."

"Reg, it needs another four of five days."

Reg handed Al the quarter ounce of cannabis and the deal was done.

The screws knew that hooch, booze and drugs were regularly traded and taken at HMP Parkhurst but they turned a blind eye. The inmates believed that they were petrified.

"Pop down to the Blue Lagoon later, Al," Reg said before leaving the cell.

"Fuck me Al, we've just got a smoke from the biggest gangster in England," Mackie said with a broad grin.

Reg Kray called his cell the Blue Lagoon and decorated the walls with pictures of Barbara Windsor, Diana Dors, Maureen Flanagan and Joe Lewis the Boxer.

Al did pop by the Blue Lagoon later that day and found Reg drinking the prison brewed hooch from a teapot and cup.

"Al, you're going to Wandsworth on a visit soon, right?"

"Yeah, Al replied.

Al had saved up twelve visiting orders so that he could be transferred to HMP Wandworth where he would be incarcerated for two weeks. Family and friends were then able to visit him every day. Secretly Al would have preferred to serve his time in Wandsworth as there was too much freedom in Parkhurst.

"Yeah, sure."

Reg Kray gave him his instructions and who to give the letter to, and to expect one in return.

One week later Al did as he was asked and hid the letter in his anal passage. Once at Wandsworth he handed the letter over and returned a letter back to Reg. Al didn't read either letter.

"Thanks Al," Reg said as he slipped the letter under his pillow.

"You don't look right," Al thought as Reg leaned in with a wry smile. *"Your eyes are gone. I've never known you to take heavy drugs and you're not on Dr Cooper's list."*

"Have they heard about us up at Wandsworth?" Peter Gillete said as Reg patted him on the head.

"Who is this little upstart?" Al thought as he looked Peter Gillete up and down.

"Ron and I are going to adopt him," Reg said.

Peter Gillete had a huge smile on his face.

"Yeah, everyone knows," Al said.

"Yeah, the Kray Twins are going to adopt me," Peter Gillete said with a smirk.

"I don't fucking like you," Al thought. *"You're a two bob nothing trying to worm your way in with proper people because Reg has a soft spot for you."*

"Peter wants to be a pop star."

"Really," Al said.

"Ron and I are going to help him."

"Look at that muggy little tosspot smiling like he's just won the pools," Al thought.

"We have connections and can make things happen."

"A pop star eh, Peter?" Al said. "So, tell me…who do you like to listen to?"

"I know that they're not everyone's cup of tea, but I do like Brotherhood of Man."

"What the fuck?" Al thought.

" 'United We Stand' was a great song."

"I don't know it," Al lied.

"Yeah and Angelo just gets everyone up and dancing. I like that."

"The only song I can think of is 'Save All Your Kisses for me'" Al said.

"Yeah, and I fucking hated that song too," Al thought.

"Peter's got a great voice," Reg said as he leant back in his Chesterfield armchair.

Al couldn't help but notice the ashtray stood a good four inches high in cigarette butts.

"I have," Peter Gillete said as he thrust his chest out.

"We're going to make him into a big pop star," Reg said.

"Good luck with that," Al said to Peter Gillete.

"Al, do you want a drop of hooch?"

Al paused for a few seconds and then nodded.

"Yeah, sure, why not."

Reg poured Al a mug of the prison brewed alcohol.

"How the hell can Reggie Kray be taken in by this creepy little mug?" Al thought as he sipped the hooch.

In 1990 a song called *'I began to Notice'* was co-written by Reggie Kray and Peter Gillete. It was recorded and released into the charts by Bold Reprive Records

***

Al passed Black George on the wing. He was having a heated argument with one of the London lads. Black George was a Yorkshire man and owned a caravan manufacturing business. He hated Londoners and was doing twelve years for robbing a hotel. Every so often, when he didn't get his medication on time, he would go off his rocker and try to kick off.

"Fucking Londoners think you have the right to run everything!"

"Not him again," Al thought as he watched a big mouthy Black Country lad known as 'Big Tony' gobbing off to a small crew of South London lads.

"All that working out in the gym is for poofs!"

"This is not going to end well," Al thought as Big Tony continued to slag off the London lads.

"What, are you all stuck up each other?" Big Tony said with a loud exaggerated laugh. "South London... I fucking shit them."

"Speak to me like that and I'd fucking smash seven sorts of shit out of you," Al thought.

Big Tony fired off several more insults before returning to his cell. Al watched as the South London lads exchanged a few words and then mobbed up and strode down the wing to Big Tony's cell. The cell door slammed shut and Big Tony was smashed to a pulp.

Two days later Big Tony was patched up and back on the wing. Davey, one of the South London crew saw him coming for him down the wing. He side stepped the big man and bolted down the wing and put himself on rule 43.

Prison Rule 43 provides segregation when the prison authorities consider it necessary to maintain good order and discipline and when inmates request it for their own protection.

Davey lost face with the South London crew.

Al met up with Mackie and Mackie's pal, Johnny Kendall.

Johnny Kendall was a professional London burglar. He had a reputation for being robust, daring and a diabolically clever criminal. Al had heard stories where Johnny had accumulated millions but couldn't resist living it up, the flash life style that brought unwelcome attention to your door. Johnny believed that he was London's King of the Burglars. He was sentenced to eight years.

"Hello Al, how's it going?" Johnny said.

"Yeah, good, you?"

"Everything is hunky dory," Johnny said with a broad smile.

"You're lying," Al thought. *"You're a nice enough fella but you can't keep that big mouth of yours shut."*

"Do you have much to do with the South London lads?"

"Why?"

"No reason, just asking."

"You've gone and upset someone and you're here trying to recruit back up," Al thought.

"They're a nice bunch of lads; we get on well."

"I know your game, Johnny," Al thought.

"I don't take any of their shit," Mackie said.

"Oh don't do it Mackie," Al thought. *"Johnny's playing you."*

"I don't know who they think they are," Johnny said directly to Mackie.

"I've seen this shit so many times," Al thought. *"This is typical prison politics. Johnny wants back up, so he's befriended Mackie and is trying to get me on side. Once he has the right numbers, it's a stand-off and then Johnny will worm his way back in with South London and tell them what Mackie and I are supposed to have said, and so the cycle repeats itself. Seen it, been there and bought the T-shirt."*

"Let me be crystal clear with you, Johnny," Al said firmly. "I like the South London lads and to be frank I don't fucking know you."

"I didn't mean anything, Al."

"Good because I have friends in here and I have no time for bollocks. I'm looking to do my bird and get the fuck out of here. Do you understand what I'm saying?"

"Yeah, I didn't mean anything."

On December 10th 1987, Johnny Kendall and Sydney Draper, while serving life imprisonment for murder, escaped from HMP Gartree in a Bell 206 long range five-seater helicopter that had landed in the exercise yard. The escape was considered the most daring in British history. Johnny Kendall was captured fifty-one days later in Chelsea, and Sydney Draper was arrested in Enfield, North London, by armed police officers fourteen months later.

Word had spread around the wing that a new con had arrived, and had had serious words with one of the older screws.

"How sure are you?" Al said.

"I'm telling you, Al, Craig heard it first hand and he told Bermondsey Kevin, who in turn told me."

"So what did he say again?"

"He strode up to the screw, looked him up and down and said 'I remember you, you bastard. Thought you was a big hard bastard back in the 60s beating me and a few of the lads to a pulp for no real reason. So listen to this, matey, your card is fucking marked and there will be payback'."

"Was that Dyson?"

"Yeah, Officer Dyson."

"He's as old as the fucking hills," Al said. "He must be close to retirement."

"Some people, especially people in places like this, have long memories."

"Did Dyson say anything?"

"Yeah, he said 'I'm a fifty four year old man and my best mate in here was stabbed on his retirement day. I don't give a flying fuck what you do or what goes on in here. I just want to get out alive'."

"What goes around comes around," Al thought. *"A prisoner with no release date has nothing to lose and nothing to fear. I wouldn't want to be in your bully boy shoes, Officer Dyson."*

Officer Dyson managed to avoid conflict with the new inmate. However, on his last day before retirement, Officer Dyson was viciously stabbed during a frenzied attack.

***

Al had become friends with a group of IRA Lads. It was shortly after the Harrods bombing in December 1983 when they first struck up a conversation. Reggie Kray was adamant that the IRA attacks on innocent Londoners, servicemen and horses was out of order. The IRA lads would never discuss business in their cells as they believed they were bugged by MI5.

"So why Celtic?" Al asked.

"We have history and a strong, unrivalled, connection Al," Winnie McGee said.

"Ireland has a history with Celtic football club?" Al asked with a quizzical expression.

"The club was actually established by an Irishman, Brother Wafrid. His aim was to help improve the conditions for the Irish immigrants."

"I didn't know that," Al thought as he listened to Winnie's history lesson.

"Celtic is far more than a football club for Irish people. Who do you support?"

"I'm a Rangers supporter through and through."

Al had learnt that the Provisional IRA was structured like a real army with ranks and a paramilitary force that sought to end British rule in Northern Ireland and facilitate Irish reunification to bring about an independent republic encompassing all of Ireland. The three men truly believed that they were at war with the British and that they were now prisoners of war.

The Provisional IRA was amongst the most highly organised and sophisticated terrorist groups in the world.

"I mean you no disrespect, Al," the IRA captain said. "But you are a criminal and we are political prisoners."

Al was fuming.

"I should fucking chin him!" Al thought.

"That's all well and good," Al hissed. "But you are all banged up in the same jail as me!"

"We will be out of here one day," Punter interrupted.

Al and Punter had become good friends.

"Do you truly believe that?"

"I don't doubt it for a second," Punter said with conviction. "The war will come to an end and we will all be released."

The IRA captain nodded his head in agreement.

"I can't ever see that happening," Al thought.

"No way," Al said as he shook his head.

"I promise you, Al McIntosh, the day will arrive when we prisoners of war will all be released and return to our homeland."

"We're not terrorists," Winnie said before sipping on his hooch. "We're freedom fighters."

"We have family and friends back at home and they understand and support our sacrifice."

"Would it not be better to just open some kind of dialogue?"

"If only it were that easy."

"They're not listening and so we have to make them listen in the only language they understand; violence and bloodshed."

Al sipped on his hooch.

"Guerrilla tactics."

"So do you have rules?"

"The IRA deems the following as punishable. Drug dealing, informing, criminal activity outside the IRA, joy riding and spreading dissent."

"No more IRA talk," the IRA captain said firmly. "Loose lips and all that."

"Yeah, sorry I was just curious."

Al and Punter drank the last of their hooch and left the cell. They returned to Al's cell and smoked a joint.

"I'm smoking dope with the IRA," Al thought as he held the delicious smoke in his lungs.

Chapter 21

"Hello mate, I wanted to pop by and ask if me running on the spot over your cell was an issue," Al said after knocking on the cell door.

"It doesn't bother me."

"I'm Al, Al McIntosh

"Hello mate, Jack Thompson."

In addition to doing one hundred press ups four times a day Al had taken to running on the spot to keep his fitness levels up.

"What are you in for?"

"GBH," Al said. "You?"

"Murder, and I'm sure you've heard it a million times but the old bill framed me."

"There are blokes serving time in here and sharing a cell with the bloke who actually pulled off the job," Al said. "So, Jack, it wouldn't surprise me what those bastards would do to get a conviction.

"Where are you from?"

Al chuckled.

"Glasgow but I'm about as London as you can get," Al said with a wry smile. "Kings Cross was my manor."

"Not a million miles from me then," Jack said as he offered Al a smoke. "I was born and bred in Peckham."

"Another South Londoner," Al thought. *"Are there any fuckers left there? Because Parkhurst is full of them."*

"What happened with you then Jack?" Al said as he declined Jack's kind offer.

Jack lit the hand rolled cigarette and inhaled deeply.

"You sure you want to hear this?"

"Yeah, why not?"

"I grew up on the Ledbury Estate just off the Old Kent Road," Jack said. "It's just down the road from the Elephant & Castle and Tower Bridge."

"I know it," Al said. "I had a mate live there and we did a bit of business with a couple of Millwall lads."

The image of Bootsie and Smudge doing a deal for cheque books with Leaky made him smile.

"Pair of good lads," Al thought.

"When you come from an area like that you pretty much start life on the back foot, so to get the things you want you have to go and get it."

"I can understand that," Al thought.

"We robbed a couple of factories and then took up ringing motors."

Al understood that ringing motors meant that a car was bought as an insurance write off and then an identical car would be stolen. The lads would then just change the number plates and VIN number.

"It was going like a dream," Jack said with a broad smile. "We were ringing two and three motors a week, and then sticking them through a car auction knowing that they'd end up with a motor trader somewhere and just get moved."

"Sounds like a nice earner," Al said.

"Yeah we would make five maybe six hundred quid a week," Jack said before drawing hard on his cigarette. "We could have done more but then that would have attracted unwanted attention. I suppose the lads looked on me as being quick witted, cunning and always thought things through to stay one step ahead of the old bill."

"How many in your crew?"

"Three including me," Jack said. "Mickey was my best mate all through school and we nicked and sold our first motor together. He was a proper mate, you know; as teenagers we talked about our dreams, aspirations and got off with plenty of birds around the area."

"I've had mates like that," Al thought.

"As time passed Mickey wanted less to do with ringing motors," Jack said. "He'd taken up with some posh sort from Penge and she fucking hated me and all us lot on the estate."

"It happens," Al said with a sigh.

"Cracking looking bird with a Page 3 body, but she looked down her nose at just about everyone."

"How did your mate meet her?"

"We were out having a few drinks up town and we've seen these two cracking looking sorts and so we've swooped in. We knew they were both posh sorts but any port in a storm if you know what I mean."

"Oh, I definitely do," Al thought.

"We've taken a taxi back to Penge," Jack said with a wry smile. "It turned out that these birds owned the house and were on holiday, so we split up and smashed the granny out the pair of them."

"Sweet," Al said.

"She may have been a posh sort but she was the fuck of the century."

"So what happened with Mickey?"

"He's only gone and fallen in love with her, and believe me, when he told her that he was out ringing motors with me, she drew a line on that."

"Funny how birds fall for who you are and then in no time try and change you."

"Tell me about it," Jack said. "I've said my good byes and that was it, but she's got her claws well and truly in my mate. Within a week he's knocked the ringing game on the head and has got a job as an apprentice printer with her uncle or something. He didn't come down the pub, hang out at the clubs... nothing."

"That can be harsh," Al said.

"Yeah but he's a mate and I respect his choices," Jack said as looked down at the smouldering cigarette. "We loved up market to better motors and were now making a comfy grand a week. It put good clobber on our backs, money in our pockets and attracted the birds."

"I remember my first grand in a week," Al thought with a silent chuckle. *"Nicking lead, what a game that was."*

"Anyway about a year has passed and I bumped into Mickey maybe two or three times and he seemed pretty happy. Look, I don't blame him for wanting to get out, but I just missed my mate."

"I can understand that." Al thought.

"Well the gavvers have kicked my front door in, dragged me out of bed and hauled me off down the old bill station."

"Been there," Al thought.

"After a lot of fucking about and mind games they tell me that Mickey was found dead in an abandoned warehouse. He was the victim of a brutal murder. I was fucking gutted. Shocked and grief stricken. Mickey was my best mate and I had just found out some slag has murdered him."

"The old bill don't give a flying fuck about the truth." Al thought. *"I've had it first-hand."*

"The gavvers tried the old good cop bad cop routine and then offered to put a good word in if I just signed a confession. They weren't listening, they were just desperate to pin the case on someone."

"Did you have any previous?"

Jack nodded.

"Usual kind of stuff," Jack said. "We had a tear up with a few lads in New Cross and I was nicked and then cautioned."

"Nothing serious then."

"No, but my brother, Denis, had a bit of form, so they were trying like fuck to stick it on me."

"Did you have an alibi?"

"Al, I was out with some little sort I'd pulled at the Cats Whiskers in Streatham. We were just having a nice private bite to eat and a bottle of wine. She was the kind of bird that needs more than a couple of half lagers to get her drawers off."

"Did she come forward?"

"She did but the old bill just brushed my alibi off as a fabrication. They wanted swift justice and they wanted my name in the frame."

"How many times have I seen and heard this?" Al thought.

"They manipulated evidence, planted false witnesses and coerced informants to testify against me. The entire legal system seemed stacked against me. I was in a battle for my liberty and charged with a crime that I didn't commit."

"You're just one in a long queue," Al thought. *"I was nearly there myself with Jackie O' Docherty.*

"There was no bail," Jack said. "I was just shipped off to the scrubs."

"What about your brief?"

"He was fucking useless," Jack said as he shook his head. "There were times when I wondered whose bloody side he was on."

"The bird came forward as a witness though, yeah?"

"Yeah, she did, but it was as if the truth was lost in the murky depths of corruption and prejudice."

"How do these bastards sleep at night?" Al thought.

"There was a journalist, Samuel something or other, who took a keen interest in the case. He visited me at the scrubs and told me that he was in the process of gathering irrefutable evidence that proved my innocence beyond any reasonable doubt. Al, I hung on to his every word. He seemed like my only hope."

"What happened?"

"The second I met with Samuel during the case, he painted a picture of corruption and the lengths to which the police had gone to frame me. Thank fuck I thought, as the truth emerged from the shadows, revealing a system that failed both me and the death of my friend Mickey."

"Did Samuel get to give evidence?"

Jack shook his head.

"I never saw him again and to make it worse it was the same judge that had put my brother away for a ten stretch."

Al clasped his lips tight together and shook his head.

"The bastard sentenced me to twenty five years."

"That's a fucking lifetime," Al thought.

"Are you appealing?"

"Yeah," Jack said with a sigh. "It's the only thing that keeps me going."

"You take care of yourself," Al said as he stepped towards the cell door.

"Yeah, be lucky," Jack said as Al strode back out onto the wing.

"Twenty five years for a crime he didn't commit," Al thought.

In the distance Al could make out an inmate running towards him.

"He's got a knife," Al thought. *"He's coming at me."*

As the inmate got closer Al could make out the look of fear on his face."

Al quickly clenched his fists.

"You're gonna get fucking hurt!" Al thought.

As the inmate got closer, Al ducked to the left and then threw an almighty right hander. The inmate was shaken and dropped down to one knee while still hiding the blade.

"Have this!" Al thought as he repeatedly kicked the con until he dropped the knife and lay on the floor.

"Come for me, you slag!" Al thought as he buried his shoe deep into the inmate's body.

"Break it up, break it up!" two screws called out as they charged towards Al.

Al immediately stepped back and threw his hands up into the air.

"Get this piece of shit back over to solitary," the more senior screw said while looking over the beaten inmate.

Al took a second step back and left his hands high in the air.

"On your way, McIntosh."

Al didn't need telling twice and promptly walked over to his friend Mackie.

"Fuck knows what I was supposed to have done to upset him," Al said to Mackie.

"The fella is a nonce, Al," Mackie said. "The dirty slag continually raped his four year old niece for four years. The screws have let him out for payback."

"If I had known he was a nonce I would have done him proper," Al hissed. "I fucking hate nonces!"

"I'd put a rope around all their necks and then kick the stool away for each and every one of them!" Al thought as he clenched his fists tightly together.

"They should bring back the death penalty especially for nonces. It'd serve as a deterrent to those low lives and prevent them committing their sick, heinous crimes," Mackie said.

Al was still kicking himself for not smashing the shit out of the nonce while he had the chance.

"Its rightful retribution," Mackie said as he watched the screws manhandle the nonce back onto his feet and frog march him down the wing. "They deserve to face the ultimate punishment."

Al was still watching the nonce until he finally left the wing.

"It would save this lot time, money and space if they just executed every last one of them."

"I'd like to see them all hang by their necks," Al said. "But it would open the door to include other serious crimes."

"Yeah."

"Yeah, how many people do you know that have been fitted up by the old bill?"

"A lot."

"Well imagine that's you, me or Jack Thompson and we're facing death for a crime we didn't commit, and yet those egotistical bastards would gladly see you go to your grave."

"I never thought about it like that."

"It ain't the system that's broken, Mackie, it's the people in it," Al said. "It's rotten to the core."

"Once an execution has taken place there is no way to rectify the error."

"Precisely," Al said. "So, when we get the opportunity we'll take care of them with our own form of justice."

"Yeah," Mackie hissed. "Cut them up good!"

"I'd still like to personally hang the low life scum," Al thought.

"What's going on over there?" Mackie said and nodded towards Reg Kray and a South London bank robber Al knew as Billy.

Al had been stunned to find a poster of Margaret Thatcher on the wall in Billy's single cell.

He watched as Billy mouthed off and Reg just stood there and took it.

"Any minute now Reg will do him," Mackie said with a hint of excitement.

Al shook his head.

"No, Reg can't retaliate and put that mug in the hospital."

"Why?"

"Reg can't get involved, he has to swallow."

"But he's Reg Kray."

"If he smashes the fuck out of Billy, that would fuck up any chances he's got of parole," Al said. "Ron is never getting out, but Reg has a chance."

"It ain't right."

"I admire Reg."

"Admire him, why?"

"It takes discipline and an incredible amount of self-control to just stand there and take that kind of shit while keeping your eye on the big prize, parole."

"Billy will pay the price."

"Almost certainly," Al thought.

Finally, Billy stormed off, shouting obscenities at the top of his voice.

"What was that all about?" Al said as Billy strode towards him.

"I fucking hate the Krays," Billy said. "Those bastards did my mate, East End Harry."

"You've taken liberties," Al said.

"Fuck him and fuck that nut-job Ron as well."

"You're out of order," Al said firmly.

"Ah bollocks."

"Don't fucking talk to me, keep your distance."

Billy turned swiftly on his heels and marched off down the wing talking to himself out loud.

Later that afternoon, while Billy was working out in the gym, one of the South London boys did Billy with a dumb bell to the face. He was left beaten and battered with a mouthful of broken teeth.

Chapter 22

"**H**ave you got a visit, Al?" Mackie said as he lit his rolled up cigarette.

"Yeah, my sister Doreen."

"That's nice," Fast Eddie said.

"What about you, Mackie?"

"Yeah, my brother and my old mum, love her."

Mackie went on to tell the lads that he had been eagerly anticipating the visit as it had been over a year since he had last seen any of his family. Mackie described feeling a sense of hope and joy and experiencing a connection to the outside world.

"I'm excited," Fast Eddie said as he rubbed his hands together.

"Yeah," Al said.

"Yeah, just imagine, right, we'll be stepping outside the confines of the prison environment and be surrounded by happy, familiar faces. I'm buzzing," Fast Eddie said with huge smile. "I'll get to hear about everything that's going on at home, on the estate and in the pub."

"You're looking for a sense of normalcy," Al thought. *"I don't blame you."*

"I feel a bit nervous to be honest," Mackie said quietly.

"I mean, what can my old mum think about her son being banged up in a place like this?" Mackie said. "She ain't getting any younger and me getting weighed off didn't help. My brother is a straight goer, which is a good thing, but it means they're constantly skint and dependent for everything when the next pound note comes in."

"I read that most people are only three months away from losing their homes."

"How do you mean?" Mackie asked.

"Well if you have a mortgage and lose your job or something bad happens, you've got about three months before they start repossession."

"Three months!" Al said. "I'm shocked."

"I could kick myself," Al thought. *"When the money was rolling in I should have bought half a dozen properties around London, done them up nice, and let them out to working girls."*

"You look a bit anxious," Al said as he turned to George.

"I am, mate." George said with a half-smile. "The thing is, we all have to put some kind of front on to appear strong and composed during the visit. None of us want to show any vulnerability or emotional distress as it would just burden friends and family further."

"I never thought about it like that," Fast Eddie said. "You're right though. It's like we're all actors walking out onto the stage to deliver the 'I'm alright, honest' message."

"He's right," Al thought. *"You can never show weakness...ever."*

That morning, while lying on his bed, Al found himself reflecting on his life's journey and how it had led him to serving ten years and being incarcerated with the most violent criminals in the country. He thought about some of the mistakes he'd made and they had almost always been when he'd been drinking heavily. Al thought about some of the many girls that had come and gone from his life, and wondered how it may have turned out if he had just made a commitment, moved out of London and gone straight. He wondered if Brian would have so easily fallen into the criminal lifestyle, and whether his brother John would have tried so hard to live up to his reputation. Al's introspection lead to a mix of emotions that included regret, guilt and a short lived desire to make amends. His thoughts moved on to when he had been sharing a cell with Benny Marvin a few years back:

The prison cell was dimly lit and Benny was sitting on the cold metal bunk. Al could almost hear his heart racing with anticipation. It had been nearly two long and agonizing years since he had last seen any of his friends or family. The high-security prison had confined him, separating him from the warmth of their embrace and the comforting familiarity of their presence. He told Al how the mere thought of their impending visit overwhelmed him, stirring up a mixture of hope, fear and frustration deep within his soul.

As the minutes ticked by, Benny told Al how his mind had wandered back to the precious memories of his past. He spoke about the joyous family gatherings at Christmas and the laughter shared with friends and the countless moments of support they had given him throughout his criminal life. Al sensed that he yearned for their reassuring touch, their soothing words and the feelings of unconditional love that had been stripped away from him for so long. Benny confessed that just as his longing had grown, so had his frustration. The weight of his heavy sentence wore him down, causing his emotions to twist and turn into a maddening storm. He told Al how the walls that had trapped him for countless days and nights were beginning to close in, suffocating his spirit and fuelling an uncontrollable rage within.

The two men had sat up when they heard the heavy footsteps echoing in the hallway outside. It seemed to Al to intensify Benny's restlessness. The feeling of anticipation reached a peak when the prison screw opened the locked door and stood in the frame, jiggling his keys. The screw signalled for Benny that the time for his long awaited reunion was almost upon him.

Al followed Benny along the wing with several other prisoners. He watched as Benny stepped into the visiting area, his eyes scanning the room, searching for familiar faces among a sea of strangers. Al smiled when he saw that Benny had spotted them; his parents and a favourite aunt. Tears welled up in his eyes as he rushed towards them, unable to contain the emotions that had consumed him for almost two years.

As Al sat down with his brother Brian, he looked over at Benny.

As he was approaching the table an overwhelming mixture of joy, sadness and frustration erupted into a chaotic tempest. The pent-up emotions, restrained for far too long, transformed into a burst of uncontrollable energy. The weight of his heavy prison sentence coupled with the intensity of his emotions overwhelmed him, blurring the line between reunion and turmoil.

Benny's fists clenched and he slammed his palms against the table, startling his family. The screws, trained to respond to any sign of aggression rushed over to restrain him while fearing an eruption of violence amongst the other inmates. Benny's desperate cries filled the room. It was a desperate plea for freedom from the emotional prison that had taken hold of his being.

Amidst the chaos, Benny's family stood frozen with shock, their faces were a mixture of concern and understanding. Al could see that they felt the depth of his pain and the overwhelming burden he had carried for far too long. Despite the fear that gripped them, they refused to let it cloud their compassion. The prison officers manhandled Benny with force, and removed him from the visiting room.

Al thought how all Benny truly wanted was a little reassurance. He wanted to be wrapped in their arms surrounded by their love and support to create a shield against the turmoil that had consumed him. Benny needed to feel solace within the embrace of his mum and dad. He needed reminding that he was not alone and that the prison walls, both physical and emotional, could be overcome with their unwavering support. Al sensed that Benny was desperate for a path to take him forward. He needed a way to reclaim his life from the darkness that had engulfed him. Benny needed to fight the demons that had plagued him and rebuild all the bridges that had been broken and rise triumphant from the depths of despair.

Benny Marvin was ghosted the following day.

The beautiful Doreen, Al's sister, had travelled down with her son to visit him after receiving a visiting order. HMP Parkhurst was a hardened category 'A' prison where security measures are stringent due to the high risk nature of the inmates.

Doreen looked at the visiting order for the tenth time to make sure she had arrived at the right day and time. The screw motioned her to step forward so they could carry out a body search and bag inspection to prevent any contraband entering the prison. Doreen wasn't carrying anything incriminating. She was then asked to provide identification to verify her identity before registering at the prison's visitor centre. One visitor, a bleached blonde, from Bermondsey was taken through to a separate room for a more in-depth search. Finally, Doreen was shown through to the visiting room filled with tables and chairs. As Doreen sat down she scanned the room and smiled at some of the other anxious visitors while vigilant prison officers looked on. There were strict rules and guidelines regarding visits, and the officers were there to ensure they were enforced.

Doreen looked over at a smartly dressed man wearing a dark suit and combed back grey hair at the next table. It was Charlie Kray.

Charlie Kray was the elder brother to the twins Ronnie and Reggie. There were just six years between them. He had been brought up, like the twins, around boxing and had often dreamt about winning the Lonsdale Belt as champion of the world. He trained seriously and eventually turned pro in his twenties. Charlie didn't have the same violent reputation as the twins, but after the murder of George Cornell he was dragged down like the rest of the Firm and sentenced to ten years for being an accessory to murder.

During the 1950s Charlie had a brief affair with Barbara Windsor from the 'Carry On' movies. He was also a confidant to Jackie Collins, Judy Garland, Sonny Liston and Christine Keeler.

Doreen lit a cigarette and inhaled the smoke before placing the cigarette in the ashtray. Finally the door opened and prisoners began to fill the room. Doreen beamed when she saw her brother.

"Hello Doreen," Al said, winking at her son.

"You're looking well," Doreen said as Al pulled out the chair and sat down.

"I like to keep myself in trim."

"How are you in yourself?"

"I'm doing okay."

Al and Doreen talked about their parents, mutual friends and what was happening around Kings Cross. She shared news about some of the challenges she had with men who promised the world and delivered nothing but disappointment. Al wasn't surprised to hear that the men who failed to meet her expectations were promptly dumped.

"Nothing's changed there then," Al thought as Doreen talked him through the failed relationships.

There were no happy childhood memories to reminisce about to lift their spirits. Not a single funny incident or significant milestone that they shared together back in Glasgow. There would be no sense of nostalgia to temporarily alleviate the stress of the prisoner – visitor situation.

"Have you thought about what you might want to do when you get out?"

"Right now, Doreen, I'm just taking it one day at a time," Al said with a broken smile.

"Yes of course."

There were a few moments of awkward silence between them.

"There are lots of changes around Kings Cross."

"Really."

"Yeah, a lot of the faces that you know have moved on, been sent to prison or ended up dead."

"I'm not surprised," Al thought as he reflected on the bloody, violent, empire he had built.

"What about you, Doreen," Al said to change the conversation. "What are your plans?"

Doreen lit her cigarette, inhaled deeply and then blew the smoke towards the ceiling.

"I want to meet a good-looking man who knows what he wants from this life and is prepared to go out and take it by any and all means possible."

"You want another king pin drug dealer then," Al thought as he listened.

"I have had enough of dreamers and useless no hopers. I need security for me and my children and a man who can provide that."

"So top of the list is what can a man provide financially for me," Al thought. *"So you don't want somebody that you can share open and honest conversations with, or a person that will trust and respect you as a person. Kindness and appreciating your individuality, opinions and boundaries are all just secondary. What of emotional intimacy and a connection that leads to closeness and a sense of security and bonding at a much deeper level? No, Doreen, you want what you always want... someone to pay for the lifestyle you believe you deserve."*

"Excuse me Al," Reggie Kray said. "Is this your sister?"

Al sat back.

"Hello Reg," Al said. "Yes this is Doreen, my sister, and her son."

Reggie Kray shook Doreen's hand warmly.

"It's very nice to meet you Doreen, I'm Reg."

Doreen blushed.

"Yes, Mr Kray, I know who you are."

Reggie then patted her son's head and winked.

"Please, call me Reg."

Al could see that Doreen was clearly both excited and nervous as she looked up at Reg as he spoke.

Al turned to Charlie Kray who rolled his eyes before shaking his head.

"I've always been a big supporter of you and your brother Ron," Doreen said.

"This might be the first time I've ever seen you overwhelmed," Al thought as he watched his sister expressing her admiration for Reg while showering him with compliments.

"It's been an absolute delight meeting you Doreen," Reg said as he stood up and stepped back.

"The pleasure has been all mine," Doreen said, blushing.

"Reg, Reg," another inmate called out. "Would you mind saying hello to my wife?"

Reg beamed.

"Me next, please Reg," another inmate said. "My girlfriend has always wanted to meet you."

"Reg, my dad would love to meet you."

"Reg, could you please say hello to my son."

Al noticed a huge change in the Reggie Kray that he had encountered out on the wing. It was as if being surrounded by enthusiastic fans of the Kray legend had triggered a sense of nostalgia. He moved like a superstar between the tables sharing short stories about his time in the limelight. Al watched as Reggie soaked up the adulation.

"What a wonderful man," Doreen said as she watched him kiss a prisoner's mother.

"Yeah, he's a nice guy."

"The wives and girlfriends in here all have their eyes on Reg," Al thought as he watched Reg glide effortlessly from one table to another. *"This must be some kind of validation for his former status as one of the Lords of the criminal underworld. I wonder what kind of emotions he's feeling right now, because I can see the years just falling off him with every interaction."*

Charlie nodded to Al.

"He always does this," Charlie said as he sat back in his chair.

"He's a celebrity, a household name," Al said.

"This must be reaffirming Reggie's belief that he and his brother must have had a significant impact on people's lives, and that the good they had done while climbing their way to the top of the criminal underworld must have been appreciated," Al thought. *"It must be uplifting for Reg, having been handed out such a severe prison sentence, that he hasn't just been forgotten, and the infamy of the Kray name still lives on."*

Al and Doreen watched as the criminal legend shook hands, greeted young children warmly, and kissed the ladies. Reggie Kray was back in the public eye and he needed no time to adjust to the overwhelming presence of fans and the memories it resurfaced.

"I can't believe I've just met Reggie Kray," Doreen said.

Reg appeared genuinely touched by the interaction between him and the inmates' visitors. The atmosphere in the visitor's room was brimming with gratitude, enthusiasm and a powerful deep connection created by Reg and his fans.

"Reggie Kray you are a superstar," Al thought as he watched Reg sign autographs while reinforcing his celebrity status.

"I've got some sad news, Al," Doreen said, lowering her head.

"What? What is it?"

Doreen began to shake her head slowly.

"This isn't easy."

"Just spit it out," Al said firmly.

"It's your friend, Mae West."

"What about Mae?"

Al was concerned.

"Mae is dead."

"What?"

"I'm sorry Al."

"What happened?" Al said as he clenched his fists.

"Mae died of Aids."

The human immunodeficiency virus are two species of Lentivirus that infect humans. Over time they cause Acquired Immunodeficiency Syndrome (Aids), a condition in which progressive failure of the immune system allows life-threatening, opportunistic infections and cancer to thrive.

Al slumped back into his seat, having been hit square on with a myriad of emotions.

"I'm in shock," Al thought as Doreen's words played over and over in his head. *"I can't believe it…Aids!"*

"Are you sure?"

Doreen nodded her head.

"It might just be gossip or someone making up shit," Al said. "You know how people can be."

"No, I'm sorry Al, but it's true."

"This is crazy!" Al thought. *"Mae can't be dead, not my good friend Mae West."*

"I can't believe it." Al said as he shook his head.

Al felt an overwhelming sense of loss.

The visiting time came to an end, Charlie Kray had chatted with Al and Doreen, but finally the time had come for the inmates to return to their lives as prisoners while visitors left with stories to tell family, friends and colleagues.

***

Al returned to his cell; he was devastated that his friend was dead. As he lay back on his bed he felt overwhelmed and a deep sense of loss.

"It wasn't that long ago that Brian, Leaky and I sorted out those loan sharks you got involved with," Al thought as tears began to stream down his cheeks.

Just before Al was arrested, he learnt that Mae West had a heart attack. He had linked Mae's condition to the loan sharks, so Leaky, Brian and Al went to their premises and gave them a good hiding and a stern warning to stay away from Mae West. When Al visited Mae in hospital he was extremely angry with Al for getting involved because he didn't want him to serve time on his behalf. 'You're not a fourteen-year-old boy anymore' were the last words Mae had said to him.

"I'm never going to see Mae again," Al thought as he struggled to hold the tears back. *"You were so good to me. I wouldn't have survived without your kindness."*

Al wiped the tears away but they persisted. The grief Al was experiencing was unlike anything he had experienced before.

"You were my friend," Al thought as turned over and buried his head deep into the pillow. *"I will miss you."*

Al cried over the loss of his friend for most of the night. Reg Kray came to his cell in the morning and offered his condolences when he heard the news. Al thought that was an extremely thoughtful thing to do.

The day passed by with Al reflecting on the memories he shared with his friend and the impact Mae had on his life. He experienced moments of helplessness and even guilt while questioning if there was something he could have done or changed so that Mae would still be alive.

Al returned to his cell. He needed support and empathy, but prison was not a place where he would receive either of those, so he opted for space to process his emotions.

One week later:

It was still dark outside when Al woke up in his cell.

"Something isn't right," Al thought as he turned over and closed his eyes. *"I don't know what it is, but my gut feeling tells me that something isn't right."*

Al felt a heightened sense of anticipation as if something significant was on the horizon.

"It's just another day," Al told himself.

Being a category A prisoner, Al had become attuned to his surroundings with all his senses being on high alert. He would spot activity out on the wing that told him something was about to kick off and nine times out of ten he had been right. Surviving prison life had significantly heightened his awareness and made him more perceptive and observant to his environment.

Al was becoming increasingly restless.

"I can't shake this feeling off," Al thought, experiencing a fluttery feeling in his stomach and a quickening of his heartbeat.

"Fuck it, I can't just lie here like this," Al thought as he sat up and twisted around with his feet placed firmly on the floor.

Al felt a surge of energy wash over his body. He clenched both fists.

"This is getting silly," Al thought as he slowly unclenched his fists.

Al leapt up onto his feet, scratched his manhood and then dropped down to the floor and began to do press ups.

"1,2,3,4,5,6,7,8,9" Al thought as he allowed his nose to touch the cold concrete floor before pushing himself back up. *"10,11,12,13,14,15."*

Al had relied on his instincts from an early age, so nothing was going to push away the feeling that something wasn't right. His mental strength came from a strong belief in his abilities, supported by a powerful gut instinct.

"95,96,97,98...100!"

Al leapt up onto his feet and shook his arms and hands.

As he sat back on the bed, he remembered being a young boy living in the shadows of the tenements in Glasgow. At an early age he had become known by the local lads as a fearless villain and was respected by both his friends and enemies. With a piercing gaze and calculating mind, he orchestrated daring warehouse heists while leaving no trace behind. Al's reputation had been built on his intellect, but little did he know that his gut instincts would soon become his greatest asset.

One moonlit night, Al and his friends received word of an unprecedented opportunity. There was a houseful of stolen lead and metal door handles. A rival gang had stored it and left two lads as guards. The challenge had excited him, but there was a lingering doubt in his mind.

Al planned his assault meticulously; he had walked the area, checked out the other houses awaiting demolition nearby, and gathered information on the rival gang's movements. However, his instincts grew stronger, whispering cautionary words in his ear. Doubts began to cloud Al's confidence and yet he pushed them aside as he imagined cashing in the haul.

On the eve of the robbery he and his two friends moved cautiously around the perimeter of the house. He approached the downstairs kitchen window on his knees, but as he got closer his gut instincts screamed out at him, urging him to stop. It had been a rare moment of uncertainty for Al. He rose slowly and then quickly peeked through the window. The room appeared deserted with no visible signs of danger, and yet the voice in his head nagged on. Al stepped back to reassess the situation, and just as he did, he heard a match strike and the light from the flame lit up several young lads standing in the dark holding knives and iron bars.

Al took a sharp intake of breath and held out his hand to his friends. At that moment he realised the true power of his gut instincts, and from then onwards he vowed to trust them. The rival gang had tried to set him and his friends up. The trap would have almost certainly meant death for him.

In later years the effects of alcohol created a blur between feelings, but while sober they were his guiding light in a dangerous world full of shadows.

Al could hear the echo of shuffling boots outside his cell.

"Screws!" Al thought. *"Am I due a kicking?"*

Al clambered off the bed and stood upright. He was ready for whatever came his way.

The locks clicked and turned and the cell door opened.

"McIntosh, get your gear together... you're on the move!"

Books by Al McIntosh

With Dean Rinaldi

Villain No Remorse

Villain No Remorse II

Villain No Remorse III

Villain No Remorse IV

Coming Soon

In 2025 Al McIntosh embarks on the first of his historical fiction novels:

The Glaswegian & The Rope

Contact:

Facebook: Al McIntosh Author

www.almcintosh.com

Facebook: Georgian, Victorian and Edwardian Crime

Facebook: Dean Rinaldi Ghostwriter Publisher Mentor.

www.deanrinaldi-ghostwriter.com

Printed in Great Britain
by Amazon